The Year of the Poet XI

August 2024

The Poetry Posse

inner child press, ltd.
'building bridges of cultural understanding'

The Poetry Posse 2024

Gail Weston Shazor
Shareef Abdur Rasheed
Teresa E. Gallion
hülya n. yılmaz
Noreen Snyder
Tzemin Ition Tsai
Elizabeth Esguerra Castillo
Jackie Davis Allen
Mutawaf Shaheed
Caroline 'Ceri' Nazareno
Ashok K. Bhargava
Alicja Maria Kuberska
Swapna Behera
Albert 'Infinite' Carrasco
Michelle Joan Barulich
Eliza Segiet
William S. Peters, Sr.

~ * ~

In order to maintain each poet's authentic voice, this volume has not undergone the scrutiny of editing. Please take time to indulge each contributor for their own creativity and aspirations to convey their uniqueness.

hülya n. yılmaz, Ph.D.
Director of Editing ~
Inner Child Press International

General Information

The Year of the Poet XI
August 2024 Edition

The Poetry Posse

1ˢᵗ Edition : 2024

This Publishing is protected under Copyright Law as a "Collection". All rights for all submissions are retained by the Individual Author and or Artist. No part of this Publishing may be Reproduced, Transferred in any manner without the prior **WRITTEN CONSENT** of the "Material Owners" or its Representative Inner Child Press. Any such violation infringes upon the Creative and Intellectual Property of the Owner pursuant to International and Federal Copyright Laws. Any queries pertaining to this "Collection" should be addressed to Publisher of Record.

Publisher Information
1ˢᵗ Edition : Inner Child Press
intouch@innerchildpress.com
www.innerchildpress.com

Copyright © 2024 : The Poetry Posse

ISBN-13 : 978-1-961498-37-2 (inner child press, ltd.)

$ 12.99

WHAT WOULD LIFE BE WITHOUT A LITTLE POETRY?

Dedication

This Book is dedicated to

Humanity, Peace & Poetry

the Power of the Pen

can effectuate change!

&

The Poetry Posse

past, present & future,

our Patrons and Readers &

the Spirit of our Everlasting Muse

*In the darkness of my life
I heard the music
I danced . . .
and the Light appeared
and I dance*

Janet P. Caldwell

Table of Contents

Foreword	*ix*
Preface	*xiii*
Renowned Poets	*xv*
Lĭ Bái	

The Poetry Posse

Gail Weston Shazor	1
Alicja Maria Kuberska	9
Jackie Davis Allen	15
Tezmin Ition Tsai	23
Shareef Abdur – Rasheed	29
Noreen Snyder	39
Elizabeth Esguerra Castillo	45
Mutawaf Shaheed	51
hülya n. yılmaz	57
Teresa E. Gallion	63
Ashok K. Bhargava	69
Caroline Nazareno-Gabis	75

Table of Contents . . . *continued*

Swapna Behera	81
Albert Carassco	89
Michelle Joan Barulich	95
Eliza Segiet	101
William S. Peters, Sr.	107

August's Featured Poets — 117

Ibrahim Honjo	119
Khalice Jade	127
Irma Kurti	139
Mennadi Farah	145

Inner Child Press News — 155

Other Anthological Works — 197

Foreword

Renowned Poets

Lǐ Bái

In this August Issue offering of the Year of the Poet, we bring you Li Bai, eminent Chinese Poet. Li Bai, also known as Li Po, remains one of the most revered figures in Chinese literature, celebrated for his profound contributions to Tang dynasty poetry. Born in 701 AD during a time of cultural flourishing and political complexity, Li Bai's life and work encapsulate the spirit of an era marked by artistic innovation and philosophical inquiry. His poetry, characterized by its emotional depth, vivid imagery, and mastery of language, transcends time and cultural boundaries, resonating with readers both in China and around the world.

As an itinerant poet, Li Bai's experiences influenced his writing, recording not only the beauty of the natural world but also the nuances of human emotion and the longing for freedom. His unique style and bold themes often challenged conventions and invited readers to explore the interplay between nature and the self. This article delves into the life of Li Bai, his literary achievements, and the lasting legacy of his work, exploring why he continues to inspire generations of poets and admirers alike. Through an examination of his most notable poems and the historical context in which he wrote, we gain insight into the artistic genius of Li Bai and his profound impact on Chinese literature and culture.

Let The Poetry Posse engage your poetry readings by their wonderful, poignant pieces all depicting their own perspectives about the world we live in and their varied experiences.

My congratulations again to The Poetry Posse for coming up with another brilliant display of poetic prowess!

Elizabeth Esguerra Castillo

International Author/Poet/Visual Artist

Now Available

www.innerchildpress.com/world-healing-world-peace-poetry

Now Available

www.innerchildpress.com/the-anthology-market.php

Preface

We, **Inner Child Press International, The Year of the Poet** and **The Poetry Posse** welcome you.

WOW . . . a decade +. We continue to be excited as we have now crossed over into our 11th year of Production for **The Year of the Poet**.

This particular year we have chosen to feature renowned poets of history. We do hope you enjoy. Read ~ Learn.

For those of you who are not familiar with our story, back in 2013, a few of us poets got together with the simple intention of producing a book a month. That was our challenge. Since that time the enterprise has blossomed and brought forth a fruit that seems to keep on growing as evidenced as we enter 2023.

Our purpose is simple. Through our lyrical words and verse, we not only wish to share our poetic works, but we also have the poetic naiveté to believe that we can assist in the growth of consciousness of the things that have an effect our collective humanity. Therefore, we welcome your readership. For more about what we are attempting to accomplish, have a look at our Publishing Web Site . . . www.innerchildpress.com. If you would like to know a bit more about this particular endeavor please stop by for a visit at :

www.innerchildpress.com/the-year-of-the-poet

Over the years, Inner Child Press has been socially active to bring awareness and catalog through literature the things that have an impact upon our world and its inhabitants. We have solicited, produced, underwritten and published quite a few volumes to that end. For more insight you may wish to visit : www.innerchildpress.com/the-anthology-market. If you are a writer, poet, or activist, you would be advised to keep a eye out for upcoming volumes should you desire to participate. All readers are welcomed as well. Note, that there is a myriad of published volumes that are available as a FREE PDF download as well as available for purchase at affordable prices.

We at this time extend to you our well wishes for your own personal journey and hope that you consider including us as a travel companion.

Bless Up

Bill

William S. Peters, Sr.

Publisher
Inner Child Press International
www.innerchildpress.com

Renowned Poets
Lǐ Bái

701 ~ 762

August 2024

by hülya n. yılmaz, Ph.D.

Li Bai, with the courtesy name Taibai who rivaled Du Fu for the title of greatest Chinese poet and earned such recognition as one of the most influential poets of the Tang dynasty and in Chinese history as a whole. He regarded himself as being a part of the imperial family, but in actuality, he belonged to a lower-ranked family of the same surname.

After several nomadic years, during which time he was already composing poetry, he gained acceptance from a group of distinguished court poets at the age of 41. Two years later, he began his wanderings again. Prince Lin, the sixth son of the emperor, granted him the unofficial title of "Poet Laureate" to his military expedition when Li Bai was 55 years old. Being accused of an intent to establish an independent kingdom, the prince was executed. Li Bai was arrested and imprisoned at first, then banished to Yelang (in the present-day western Guizhou province).

A story revolves around Li Bai's death in eastern China. It is a popular belief that he died drunk by drowning while he tried to grab the moon's reflection in the water. When China's tradition of imbibers is concerned, he belonged to the most renowned wine drinkers. The fact that in his poems he celebrated the joy of drinking frequently could have been a factor in the spreading of that folk legend about his death.

"Quiet Night Thought" below is considered Li Bai's most famous poem, in which this poet's focus is not on wine drinking, but rather on nature and his contemplative tendency.

Quiet Night Thought

At the foot of my bed, moonlight

Yes, I suppose there is frost on the ground.

Lifting my head I gaze at the bright moon

Bowing my head, thinking of home.

The diversity of the themes displayed in Li Bai's poetry is reflecting on "Seeing Off a Friend".

Seeing Off a Friend

Green hills above the northern wall,

White water winding east of the city.

On this spot our single act of parting,

The lonely tumbleweed journeys ten thousand li.

Drifting clouds echo the traveler's thoughts,

The setting sun reflects my old friend's feelings.

You wave your hand and set off from this place,

Your horse whinnies as it leaves.

---

*Also known as Li Bo, Li Pai, Li Po, Li Taibai, Qinglian Jushi according to The Editors of Encyclopedia Britannica. His literary name was Qinglian Jushi.

◇ ◇ ◇ ◇

Selected Sources:

Encyclopedia Britannica
100 Tang Poems
chinese-poems.com
chinas-most-famous-poem-by-li-bai/
Wikipedia

◇ ◇ ◇ ◇

hülya n. yılmaz, Ph.D.

Professor Emerita, Liberal Arts (Penn State, U.S.A.)
Director of Editing Services, Inner Child Press International (U.S.A.)

*Poets . . .
sowing seeds in the
Conscious Garden of Life,
that those who have yet to come
may enjoy the Flowers.*

Poets, Writers . . . know that we are the enchanting magicians that nourishes the seeds of dreams and thoughts . . . it is our words that entice the hearts and minds of others to believe there is something grand about the possibilities that life has to offer and our words tease it forth into action . . . for you are the Poet, the Writer to whom the Gift of Words has been entrusted . . .

~ wsp

poetry is . . .

Poetry succeeds where instruction fails.

~ wsp

Now Available

www.innerchildpress.com/the-anthology-market.com

Gail Weston Shazor

Gail Weston Shazor

Gail Weston Shazor is a lover of words. She is fond of the arcane, unusual and the not yet words.

Coining words at an early age, there was often a bit of trouble with teachers, but she always had her mother and aunt to back up her choices in expression. Born in Mississippi, she spent her early years with her grandparents. Each of the four left very careful influences on her pre-schooling. She learned in turn how women worked in and out of the home and how men worked in and out of the home to support the family. She learned that a lack of proper schooling was not the only way to learn and understanding life was a great teacher. As in most rural families of color, women had a greater chance of formal learning. Both of Gail's grandmothers read out loud to the family whether it was the bible or the newspapers and important documents to their spouses.

Gail Weston Shazor has authored (so far) Notes from the Blue Roof, A Overstanding of an Imperfect Love, HeartSongs and Lies My Grandfather's Told Me. The number of anthologies is too many to list with the premier accomplishment of one of the contributors to The Year of The Poet. Gail will always lend her ink to community projects and will purchase the books of fellow poets in the Inner Child Press family.

Tang

In the quiet
I seek the roads
Leading from Janmin Pass
To the forever curves
Of life's travels
The brilliance of the moon
Covering the mountains
I have seen beauty
I have married beauty
From the Yellow Crane Tower
I sought more
Difficult roads
Settling on coaching
The bounty from the earth
I raise a toast
To life itself

The Measure of a Woman

What's the measure of a woman
Is it the way we move
To unheard music
Or carry the pain of indifference
Under our skin
Can you add weight to
My fingertips
To make me more sorrowful
Or even hold me to
A standard that you cannot
Bear the wanting of
Are my feelings not valid
In the day to day moments
Of the reconciliation of
Intentional hurts by others
That you view as histrionics
And thus the measure of wanting
Sits squarely on my shoulders
Should I bite my tongue
Is my waist too wide
Or my shoulders too broad
And how do you measure
The pressure of a spine
Bent under hateful words
Mitigated by the humor
And gentleness required
To hold your hand when
You need it
Some folks say we should
Be this smart
So I can fly to the moon
And still make cornbread

On the way back down
Fallen
Short
Where is the hope written
In the stars
That you would love me
Just because I am worthy
And not measured against
Another ideal of what is
Attractive
Why is the measure
Of a woman
Why is my measure
As a woman
And please tell me
Where I fall short
Of being beautiful and desired
What is the measure of a woman
And will you let the Maker know
Of his latest failure
So that I can
Be born again

Compline

Water caresses psalmody
Wearing the rough edges away
Smoothing weariness into the
Curves of the porcelain basin
A gurgling cacophony of clean
Blends with twilight cricketsong
Pooling into the deep recesses
At the hollow of my spine

The quality of my pleasure
Outweigh my need to rush
The sensual distillery of lavender
And the smell of your memory
At the bend of my knee
My heart stills to prayers
I am not daunted by unfinished chores
Nor am I troubled any longer
By the rush of daylight minutes

Quietness fits across my shoulders
Like a favorite afghan
Against the summer breeze
An anthem rich in coolness
And solemn in need
My absolution is committed
Into your breast
For I remain eager to see your hue
In iridescent hummingbird wings
And the azure of open seas

Miles stretch into dismissal
A solemnity of confession

Gail Weston Shazor

Ancient is the desire for comfort
And the completion of togetherness
I would have the feast and the rest
As I enter into this night's slumber
My soul longs to bridge the distance
And finally unite our lives
As I have committed my heart to you

Alicja Maria Kuberska

Alicja Maria Kuberska

Alicja Maria Kuberska – awarded Polish poetess, novelist, journalist, editor.

She is a member of the Polish Writers Associations in Warsaw, Poland and IWA Bogdani, Albania. She is also a member of directors' board of Soflay Literature Foundation, Our Poetry Archive (India) and Cultural Ambassador for Poland (Inner Child Press, USA)

Her poems have been published in numerous anthologies and magazines in : Poland, Czech Republic, Slovakia, Hungary,Ukraina, Belgium, Bulgaria, Albania, Spain, the UK, Italy, the USA, Canada, the UK, Argentina, Chile, Peru, Israel, Turkey, India, Uzbekistan, South Korea, Taiwan, China, Australia, South Africa, Zambia, Nigeria

She received two medals - the Nosside UNESCO Competition in Italy (2015) and European Academy of Science Arts and Letters in France (2017). Ahe also received a reward of international literary competition in Italy „ Tra le parole e 'elfinito" (2018). She was announced a poet of the 2017 year by Soflay Literature Foundation (2018).She also received : Bolesław Prus Prize Poland (2019), Culture Animator Poland (2019) and first prize Premio Internazionale di Poesia Poseidonia- Paestrum Italy (2019).

Li Bai

Immortal poet

He found the essence of the word
hidden at the bottom of the chalice.
In the city of Xuan
he completed his journey of a thousand miles.
He closed in his eyes
the beauty of the passing landscapes
and in the mouth the sweetness of wine
and the bitterness of sadness.

A brave wanderer,
an eternal one by choice
Sometimes the emperor's favourite,
sometimes an exile
but never a sycophant
or a man eager for honours
gold, court glitter, academic triumphs.

A poet banished from heaven,
created for another world.
He speaks through the ages
in the words of a thousand poems,
where realism
intertwines with romantic nature,
existence is a great adventure
and time travel.
Today his poetry takes root
in everyday speech.

Write a poem…

Let the verses
be full of peace, sadness and longing,
encourage contemplation of silence and beauty.
Let them whisper about life,
transience, eternity,
death and rebirth in the eternal cycle

Give the world a little bit of yourself.
Talk about emotions
coming from your deep inside
like sparkling wine
from a crystal goblet
full of unexpected flavour

Write a poem…

Turning around

- How is Peter feeling? – my mother asked
once again today.
- He's not well. Peter is in the hospital.
This news once again caused astonishment
and painted sadness on her pale face.

Time creaked
and changed the trajectory of movement.

She thought back to her parents,
happy moments of childhood,
the non-existent dolls and a teddy bear

She played
with the dog and the kitten again,
stole unripe fruit
from her neighbour's orchard,
and talked to the bees
and her favourite cow.

The memories faded away
and she came back to the present time.
- How is Peter feeling?
Is he okay?

There are no more dolls, teddy bears
and today.
I am sad and helpless.

Time creaked and rushed forward.

Jackie Davis Allen

Jackie Davis Allen

Jackie Davis Allen, otherwise known as Jacqueline D. Allen or Jackie Allen, grew up in the Cumberland Mountains of Appalachia. As the next eldest daughter of a coal miner father and a stay at home mother, she was the first in her family to attend and graduate from college. Her siblings, in their own right, are accomplished, though she is the only one, to date, that has discovered the gift of writing.

Graduating from Radford University, with a Bachelor's of Science degree in Early Education, she taught in both public and private schools. For over a decade she taught private art classes to children both in her home and at a local Art and Framing Shop where she also sold her original soft sculptured Victorian dolls and original christening gowns.

She resides in northern Virginia with her husband, taking much needed get-aways to their mountain home near the Blue Ridge Mountains, a place that evokes memories of days spent growing up in the Appalachian Mountains.

A lover of hats, she has worn many. Following marriage to her college sweetheart, and as wife, mother, grandmother, teacher, tutor, artist, writer, poet and crafter, she is a lover of art and antiques, surrounding herself, always, with books, seeking to learn more.

In 2015 she authored *Looking for Rainbows, Poetry, Prose and Art*, and in 2017, *Dark Side of the Moon*. Both books of mostly narrative poetry were published by Inner Child Press and were edited by hulya n. yilmaz in 2019, *No Illusions. Through the Looking Glass*, which was nominated to be considered for a Pulitzer Prize by the publisher and editor of Inner Child Press, ltd.

http://www.innerchildpress.com/jackie-davis-allen.php
jackiedavisallen.com

He Did It His Way

A man's journey, his life
Transversed by weight of time.
A troubled country, some actions,

Some consequences expected.
From body and soul, a price to pay.
So too from the mind.

Creativity, talent, a strong stirring,
Flowing like a river overflowing,
His gifts, God-given, surged within,

Without. Acknowledged or not.
He did it his way. He did it his way.
For him, it was the only way.

Adopting attire of an activist, in heat
Of self-belief, beset by the times,
Adulation soon crowned his head.

With pseudo's religious fever.
From nature's self-catharsis,
Did ever such a poet exist?

No Meeting of Minds

Down the road and across the mountain, there sat
a board and batten run-down house, its windows
forever blindfolded beneath layers of dust and smoke;
a fire of suspicious origin erupted there one night.

How great were the flames of that dear family's pain.

Its owner was an absentee landlord living high,
up near the sky in a city a thousand miles away;
He worried only about taxes, never electricity, or heat;
his accumulated wealth, the envy of Wall Street.

Unlike the little family, he always had enough to eat.

In that house, down the lane, where weeds and grass
grew strong, it was as if the green was attempting
to prevent the screams of the wronged from being seen.
Neither negligence nor regret were sufficient

to replace hope and faith, or their trust in a better day.

Who was it that came to their rescue?
The couple whose pennies filled ceramic pigs?
Or the one who counted up his largess?
The one who daily continued to balance his books

on the backs of those less fortunate?

The one who distanced himself from heart's love,
conscious?

Jackie Davis Allen

The ruined remains of the house are no more,
For in its place there sits a brand new trailer,
Grief finding the family, now decreased to three.
Today, living there on received settlement's proceeds,

life's deep scars find no recompense in dollars and cents.

Painful

Like second skin,
silent as mute
Like a hermit,
dementia resides inside

It consumes, confuses, follows, meanders
Both night and day

He wonders
as he wanders
The unexplainable,
lost; at a loss, too.

Any way to find the words to relay
What once was easy to say

His star,
once bright and keen
Has dimmed,
faded, gone away.

Still surrounding him, family and friends
Despite unknowing, despite the unknown

Jackie Davis Allen

Tzemin Ition Tsai

Tzemin Ition Tsai

Dr. Tzemin Ition Tsai comes from the Republic of China(Taiwan). In addition to being a professor of literature at a university, he is more committed to writing poems, novels, and proses. He is also an editor of "Reading, Writing and Teaching" academic text, an International editor of "Contemporary dialogues" literary periodical in Macedonia, and Vice-Chairman of the International Jury of the SAHITTO INTERNATIONAL AWARD in Bangladesh, and a columnist for "Chinese Language Monthly" in Taiwan.

In a wide range of literary creations, he is particularly fond of interesting stories or novels, and writing articles or poems about the feelings of nature and human beings. He has won many national literary awards. His literary works have been anthologized and published in books, journals, and newspapers in more than 55 countries and have been translated into more than 24 languages.

Eternal Love

At sunset, by the vast ocean's edge
I gaze upon the lifetime's splendor,
Whispers, a woman like the spring water
Her tone unique, incomparable to the sigh of ocean waves.
She exists beautifully like spring, fleeting as a butterfly,
Vanishing in a moment, every spectrum of light
Twirls my love for her into stars circling the crescent moon.

Our eyes meet, at the boundary of endless stars and sea,
Like two constant stars making a pact, blooming in the eternal sky.
She stands by the sea, tears marking her cheeks,
Wishing to know how much our love remains after parting
I follow, casting the beauty of fleeting years from my heart, even if
The Milky Way is deep, it can't stop the ripples of my profound emotions for her.
No matter where we silence ourselves, how life fades,

No matter where we silence ourselves, how life fades,
Her name burns like a torch in my heart's sea, forever undying,
The ocean's depths, like our boundless fate,
Yet life is like a candle in dreams, briefly dazzling,
Youth's fireworks extinguish, our love can only linger in the eternal,
Between the boundless heaven and earth, in that moment of meeting
Turning into a momentarily known eternity.

Fleeting Moments

Since came over autumn's embrace,
The first rays of morning light intrude in an instant.
Always, I can't tell you what feeling do it evoke in my heart?
Silently frowning, I find no way to drive them away.
Suddenly arriving, new scenes, old memories—
Alone quietly pass through the curtain,
Musing on how to block the gentle glow on the desk.
A cold night left the remaining coffee no longer steaming.
Between the pages, a bookmark records last night's chapters,
As whispered words passed half the night, unaware of ghostly visitations.

Time seems to have stopped.
All noise is isolated outside, only
Inner thoughts, with the outside breeze,
Lightly dance, past moments.
No longer stirring the slightest ripple of remembrance.
Now, nostalgic thoughts shift inward,
All worldly worries turn into ephemeral, unattached yearnings,
Becoming so small and insignificant.
Outside, birds sing urgently,
Flowering branches teasingly sway, exuding a fragrant allure.

Village Maiden's Charming Attire

Before the village, willows shimmer in green,
By the brook, apricot blossoms subtly blush,
Capturing all the spring breezes.
The village maiden, so elegantly adorned,
Seems to mourn only for fallen petals,
Her collar brushes against lotus stems,
Her gentle voice beckons passersby,
Who shyly respond with a smile.

Fearful it might be an early report of spring,
Sitting to hear frogs' calls,
The old pine tree seems to forget its autumn hues,
Listening not to the stream's shallow dance.
Reflections beneath the water, wild bamboo roots and tendrils,
Before the village, the wind dances with green strands,
Embroidered shoes lightly step, wafting fragrant winds,
A slight frown exudes charm, a smile intoxicates the soul.

The village maiden weaves dreams diligently,
A peasant girl painting rural scenes,
Touched by the red dust but not marred by dust,
The village path's floral shadows bask in warm spring light,
Her smile as fragrant as blossoms.
Why offer you lotus-scented wine on a thin grass bank?
I see the solitary water flow eastward,
Thinking of the mist and rain by the bridge,
Thinking countless times.
If not for encountering the village maiden so charmingly adorned,
Where else could one listen to the flute's melody?

Shareef Abdur Rasheed

Shareef Abdur Rasheed

Shareef Abdur-Rasheed, AKA Zakir Flo was born and raised in Brooklyn, New York. His education includes Brooklyn College, Suffolk County Community College and Makkah, Saudi Arabia. He is a Veteran of the Viet Nam era, where in 1969 he reverted to his now reverently embraced Islamic Faith. He is very active in the Islamic community and beyond with his teachings, activism and his humanity.

Shareef's spiritual expression comes through the persona of "Zakir Flo". Zakir is Arabic for "To remind". Never silent, Shareef Abdur-Rasheed is always dropping science, love, consciousness and signs of the time in rhyme.

Shareef is the Patriarch of the Abdur-Rasheed Family with 9 Children (6 Sons and 3 Daughters) and 41 Grandchildren (24 Boys and 17 Girls).

For more information about Shareef, visit his personal FaceBook Page at :

https://www.facebook.com/shareef.abdurrasheed1
https://zakirflo.wordpress.com

Dive in Wine Lake

Li Bai
B:701 AD D: 762 AD
Tang China

genius poet one of
China's greats
loved life's priceless
gifts abundantly
distributed
wind, wine, flowers, wine
sun, wine, moon, wine
mountains, wine
valleys, wine, trees, wine
yes, as Li loved life
Li loved wine
as he wrote of life
he wrote of wine
wrote of friends, wine
Li loved life to the fullest
and drank to it to the fullest
wrote creation its beauty,
pleasures being with friends
drinking with friends
looking at the moon alone
drinking wine alone
where's my friends
long gone
solitude hangs over
still drink is plenty
wrote of "Waking from
Drunkenness on a Spring
Day" Being in the Wine"
he wrote of many aspects

of life in a unique style
that endeared him to his
wine guzzling public
this genius Li Bai
said to while drunk
reach from his boat
to hold the moon's reflection
and drowned

like holding water..,

in your hands
so is the sand
passing through hour glass
so is the present as it relates to the
past
goes oooh sooo ~~fast~~
and you remember yesterday like today
though it may be 40,50 years ago today
as the creator of time say:
" By the measure of time, verily man is at loss
except those who believe in Allah and come
together in the mutual teachings of truth,
patience and constancy " *
rehearse the verse, be aware, adhere, hear
and obey
contemplate what the wahi** say
how quickly today is yesterday
how you can remember 40,50 years
like it's today
you see yourself and those there
that long since passed away
you hear them talk 50 years ago like it's today
like 50 years from now someone will hear you
long since passed away back 50 years
like it was today your standing there
the miracle that is the mind works that way
memory amazing memory, how the mind functions
science can not explain the unseen
man can only understand what anything means
if the creator says " Be " and bestow as he please
who he wants to know but not so if he says no
just the miracle of the mind's brain flow

is enough for you and i to know
it takes the masterplan of other then man to
make that so
please while we're alive, strive to be of those that time
will not render at loss

Shareef Abdur Rasheed

Like Dark Clouds..,

bring rain, pain can bring gain
thus mankind must refrain
from lusting for comfort as
struggle remains here to stay
until end of days we must embrace
another way that includes being
resolute to endure what pain comes
our way with faithful patience
each and every day
increases faith, strength, endurance
adherence to commandments
from lord of all worlds
pain purges impurities when absorbed
patiently
remembering what comes after difficulty
ease, twice as much as the pain is ease
manifests merciful reward for passing
a test
comes only from merciful lord who's
majesty and mercy stands far
above the rest who may profess to be the best
though creation can not even be an imitation
of thee creator's all-encompassing domination
as this short life no matter what's acquired
can not save you from the hour of his power
as you take your final breath
everything man-made will fade just as all
mankind has limited days to tarry
nothing here will you take to the eternal
destination but the deeds compiled
to be weighed on the scale, then only
divine mercy will determine if you passed
or failed.

either way pass or fail what comfort that
you sought to soothe will desert you and in
comparison what award awaits the faithful
earthly comfort pales, as your efforts failed
thus universal law made plain to all of us
No pain, No gain

Shareef Abdur Rasheed

Noreen Snyder

Noreen Snyder

Noreen Ann Snyder has been writing since she was a teenager. She writes a variety of different topics. Her favorite poetic forms are Sonnets, Blitz, Haiku, Tanka, and Free Verse. She always learning different poetic forms.

Noreen Ann Snyder is a poet, writer, and an author of five books, (four books are co-authored with her late husband, Garry A. Snyder.) Her poetry is in several Inner Child Press Anthologies. She is the founder of The Poetry Club on Facebook.

Li Bai

Li Bai, a talented Romantic Chinese poet
of the Tang Dynasty,
who spent most of his life as a wanderer.
He left behind a legacy of
masterpieces,
'Quiet Night Thought" was one of them.
He wrote about nature, war and death,
and of being alone far away from
his family and friends.

Peeling Potatoes

You say it's KP Duty
in the military
but I say no.
It's romantic
when you lend a helping hand,
we peel and cut up
potatoes together.
Now and then, I glimpse
at you smiling at me
and I smile back.
Oh, how romantic it is
when we do it together.

Afterthought- Now won't this make
the military Sergeants cry.

Tune of Silence

The full moon shining on earth

the stars twinkling

and smiling

as you took my hand

we waltzed to the tune

of silence;

just music in our minds.

We didn't mind for we're still in

love after all these years.

Elizabeth E. Castillo

Elizabeth Esguerra Castillo

Elizabeth Esguerra Castillo is a multi-awarded and an Internationally-Published Contemporary Author/Poet and a Professional Writer / Creative Writer / Feature Writer / Journalist / Travel Writer from the Philippines. She has 2 published books, "Seasons of Emotions" (UK) and "Inner Reflections of the Muse", (USA). Elizabeth is also a co-author to more than 60 international anthologies in the USA, Canada, UK, Romania, India. She is a Contributing Editor of Inner Child Magazine, USA and an Advisory Board Member of Reflection Magazine, an international literary magazine. She is a member of the American Authors Association (AAA) and PEN International.

Web links:

Facebook Fan Page

https://free.facebook.com/ElizabethEsguerraCastillo

Google Plus

https://plus.google.com/u/0/+ElizabethCastillo

China's Immortal Poet

Li Bo, an important poet of the Tang Dynasty

Wandered to the Yangtze River Valley

Had a colorful life, overcame strife

His verses depict his life

Full of imagery and conversational tone

Became an immortal poet

The epitome of Chinese poetry.

Loving In Silence

At times, I'd like to utter "I Love You" to you
But I know they're the three most important words that's hardest to say when it's true,
Words become empty, senseless, emotionless
When you gather the courage to speak them up,
But you can't prove it otherwise.

I chose to love you in silence
For I know in doing this, I will feel no pain,
It's only me who knows the raging feelings I kept inside
There's no rejection loving you from afar.

Supernova in the Night Sky

People come into our lives to hold up a mirror,
A reflection of who we truly are
Illuminating the beauty that already resides in us
Some can be iconic sparks of enlightenment,
To help us sing back the lost melody in our hearts
When mere words have gone mad and the rhythm drums a different beat.
There are simply those who amplify the light,
And reflect where it originated from- the Source
The angel in the night who rescues us from the darkness,
Teaching us to love ourselves once more,
And to bring out the Empathic Soul in us.
The magical moment when you open yourself up to connect the Cosmic Dots,
When the alchemical marriage of the Divine Feminine and the Sacred Masculine takes. place
And this paves the way for you to embrace your Higher Self- a destined conduit to the stars,
The supernova in the night sky where you witness a crusade of fireflies with wings emitting Pure Light,
This is when the Legend of a New World takes its daring, mystic flight!

Mutawaf Shaheed

Mutawaf Shaheed

C. E. Shy has been writing since the seventh grade. He continued writing through high school, until he became more involved in sports. After his graduation, he worked at the White Motors Company where he wrote for the company's newspaper. He started a column called: "The Poet's Corner." That was his first published work.

www.innerchildpress.com/c-e-shy.php

Taking it All Insight

Sometimes waking from stupors,
only to superimpose what his mind
saw from being on higher ground.

Sounds brought from unsung songs
that lasted only for one night. Words
created from conflict, put in the wrong
places.

Staggering up winding roads while
poems form a pathway back to sobriety
connected to society, where certain
 behavior was expected.

Normal ideas were rejected, the ones
viewed through rose tinted glasses.
Falling in and out of favor became a
labor of love, kind a like…

His mind probably wrote more than his
hands. Never considering how high and
fast time flies. He pulled his pen from it's
quiver and began to spell it all out.

Searching

My words went missing and
got tangled up in the thickets.
They got involved with fleas
and flies. They got lost in the
weeds.
My thoughts couldn't find them.
They slipped and fell as they tried
to hide. They were lost.
All the time they were looking
for me.

Mutawaf Shaheed

Thinking that, that's for me.

Knowing that it couldn't be.
Wishing that it only could.
Knowing that it would do no good.
Crying till my eyes turn pale.

Tears enough for a boat to sail.
With this burden on my heart.
It has driven life and I apart.
But only if I, could physically cry;

If I did, it would be a lie.
My spirit now accepts the fact, as it always does;
It could never be, because it never was.

hülya n. yılmaz

hülya n. yılmaz

Of Turkish descent, hülya n. yılmaz [sic] is Professor Emerita (Penn State, U.S.A.), Director of Editing Services (Inner Child Press International, U.S.A.), and a trilingual literary translator. Before her poetry and prose publications, she authored an extensive research book in German on cross-cultural literary influences.

Her works of literature include a trilingual collection of poems, memoirs in verse, prose poetry, short stories, a bilingual poetry book, and two books of poetry (one, co-authored). Her poetic offerings appeared in numerous anthologies of global endeavors.

hülya writes creatively to attain and nourish a comprehensive awareness for and development of our humanity.

hülya n. yılmaz, a traveler on the journey called "life" . . .

Writing Web Site
https://hulyanyilmaz.com/

Editing Web Site
https://hulyasfreelancing.com

Saki, Give Me the Cup!

A tavern
19th century
In comes a middle-aged man,
Takes a seat enthusiastically,
And signals to the boy, the wine-bearer:
"O Saki, o Saki, fill a large cup of wine for me!"

One of the regulars, mystified:
"How did he know our Saki?"
Another frequent customer, self-composed:
"Don't you know? He is Li Bai."
"So?" An elderly wonders out loud.
"A great poet from China. He wanders occasionally."

Wine goblets raised, all at once:
"Welcome to our part of the world, Li Bai!"

Mom and Dad

Alcoholic beverages
On Mesnevi Street
Apartment #6
Were aplenty.

Dad had a large collection.
Not that he drank a lot, no!
Our guests were always pleased.

My brother and I, of mature age,
Tasted the different liquors
Before Mom and Dad.

So that
We won't be tempted
To try them whenever with friends.

Their strategy worked superbly,
To which my daughter could attest.
Her father and I followed Mom and Dad
In their footsteps. She is a Mom herself now.
When her little precious darlings are old enough,
She might also teach them what my brother and I
Learned long before this day:
Home is the best place for everything.

A Drunk's Death, Or?

Trying to seize the moon's reflection?
On a boat? At nighttime? On open water?

What was going through his mind?
Or, did people weave their yarn of fantasy into the story?

Perhaps he, indeed, died peacefully
In the house of a relative, as some claim to this day.

Teresa E. Gallion

Teresa E. Gallion

Teresa E. Gallion was born in Shreveport, Louisiana and moved to Illinois at the age of 15. She completed her undergraduate training at the University of Illinois Chicago and received her master's degree in Psychology from Bowling Green State University in Ohio. She retired from New Mexico state government in 2012.

She moved to New Mexico in 1987. While writing sporadically for many years, in 1998 she started reading her work in the local Albuquerque poetry community. She has been a featured reader at local coffee houses, bookstores, art galleries, museums, libraries, Outpost Performance Space, the Route 66 Festival in 2001 and the State of Oklahoma's Poetry Festival in Cheyenne, Oklahoma in 2004. She occasionally hosts an open mic.

Teresa's work is published in numerous Journals and anthologies. She has two CDs: *On the Wings of the Wind* and *Poems from Chasing Light*. She has published three books: *Walking Sacred Ground, Contemplation in the High Desert* and *Chasing Light*.

Chasing Light was a finalist in the 2013 New Mexico/Arizona Book Awards.

The surreal high desert landscape and her personal spiritual journey influence the writing of this Albuquerque poet. When she is not writing, she is committed to hiking the enchanted landscapes of New Mexico. You may preview her work at

http://bit.ly/1aIVPNq or ***http://bit.ly/13IMLGh***

River of Stars

The sun sets on the river.
Moon beams send light streamers
across the water.

We become one with the light.
In the cool wave of darkness,
holding our souls close.

We hum a reverent tune
to honor the presence
of Li Bai dancing on stars.

Red wine floats from his lips
to yours in the flavor
of the season we call love.

To Be You

A tender heart and a pure soul
comes with loving too intensely.
You may be temporarily broken
by souls not able to deal with you.

Respect them and move on.
Do not intrude on their space.
You must learn to be yourself.
That is your super talent.

Always help someone on your pathway.
Embrace each one with compassion.
Each contributes to healing
your broken pieces.

Teresa E. Gallion

Dinner of Words

Cup your lips around the words.
Chew slowly to experience full flavor.
Swallow the blended words
and savor the wonderful taste
as it rolls over the back of your tongue.

Enjoy a dinner of words.
Divine flavors blend to tease
and fill the stomach of your soul.

Only a word chef may compete
for your taste buds.
Only biting verbs will make the cut
and dribble down your shirt.
The stains form unspoken art.

Reserved divine word shelves
will be able to catch words
and release phrases that massage souls.

A peasant wordsmith may miss
this mystical experience.
Her mouth will be wide open
ready to take in any word crumbs
filled with endless possibility.

Ashok K. Bhargava

Ashok K. Bhargava

ASHOK BHARGAVA is a poet, writer, inspirational speaker and a literary consultant. He has attended poetry conferences in Italy, Turkey, India and Philippines. His latest book "Riding the Tide" about his battle with cancer has been translated and published in Arabic, Hindi, Telugu and Bengali languages. He is a contributing writer to several anthologies worldwide including World Poetry Almanac 2014. He has been published in numerous print and online magazines.

Ashok has won many accolades including Poet Ambassador to Japan, Kalidasa International award, World Poetry Lifetime Achievement award, Writers Beyond Borders Peace award and Tapsilog Leadership award for his community involvement. He is founder of Writers International Network Canada Society to discover, nourish, recognize and celebrate writers, poets and artists and to assist them to network with the community at large. He is the author of eight books of poetry and one anthology. He is Artist-in-Residence at Moberly Arts & Cultural Centre and also co-edits the literary section of The Link Newspaper.

To Li Bai

My sweet delicious
wine glass is full
like my life
full of Now
full of this moment.
I drink it to my fill
without fear
of this moment
going out it's relevance.

I empty out my glass
it can't pour out wine
anymore
I keep my Now
within my heart.

Morning Walk

Wind, dreamy notes, sings
its lullaby, gently touching the leaves.
I let myself be, seduced, immersed
in song like grass.

Air shivers
and cools my fevered face
wrapped in desire.
Clouds drift by, scatter white,
sun-stolen light.

The old acacia
leaves silence
a trembling tangle of leaves.
The scents of the earth rise, climb
and then fall back to me.

Rover and Wayfarer

In the boundless cosmos,
From infinity we come,
To eternity we continue.

By a mere chance, we meet
Like drifting leaves
During the short journey of our lives.

Happy days and merry times,
We share laughter and dreams.
When sad and low, we share our sorrows.

We go away,
When the time of separation comes,
Leaving behind a memory or two.

We hope our paths will meet cross again
In the morrows,
Though we do not know.

We have our own roads to follow
And journeys to complete.

Today
The rivers flow in our eyes
But tonight
Stars will shine
In our loving hearts.

Caroline 'Ceri Naz' Nazareno Gabis

Caroline 'Ceri' Nazareno-Gabis

Caroline 'Ceri Naz' Nazareno-Gabis, author of Velvet Passions of Calibrated Quarks, World Poetry Canada International Director to Philippines is a multi-awarded poet, editor, journalist, educator, peace and women's advocate. She believes that learning other's language and culture is a doorway to wisdom.

Among her poetic belts include **Gabrielle Galloni Memorial Panorama International Youth Award** 2022, Panorama Youth Literary Awards 2020, 7th Prize Winner in the 19th, 20th and 21st Italian Award of Literary Festival; Writers International Network-Canada ''Amazing Poet 2015'', The Frang Bardhi Literary Prize 2014 (Albania), Poet Journalist Award 2014 (Tuzla, Istanbul, Turkey) and World Poetry Empowered Poet 2013 (Vancouver, Canada). She's a featured member of Association of Women's Rights and Development (AWID), The Poetry Posse, Galaktika Poetike, Asia Pacific Writers and Translators (APWT), Axlepino and Anacbanua. Her poetry and children's stories have been featured in different anthologies and magazines worldwide.

Links to her works:

http://panitikan.ph/2018/03/30/caroline-nazareno-gabis/

https://apwriters.org/author/ceri_naz/

http://www.aveviajera.org/nacionesunidasdelasletras/id1181.html

Immortal Poet
(Li Bai)

The gentle autumn wind,
Blow ripened dark clouds,
A heavy downpour
On your grave,
A Hundred thousand poets
Weep upon the fields
Of erudite and esoteric
Lamentations and poetic hums
Of genius Li Bai.
A rebellion and imperial army
Up to the modern worlds' play
On romance, war and natural beauty.
Your words are like Emperor's legacy.

Gentle Hearts

Hear the silence of the dawn,
Where whispers of light begin,
Gentle hearts beat in rhythm,
They pulse with kindness, a silent song,
Like the gentle flipping wings of a butterfly.
Gentle hearts, like petals under the sun,
They bloom with compassion,
Painting the world with hues of love.
Gentle hearts listen to the stories untold,
To someone's misfortunes and fears,
They hold larger space for your tears,
Gentle hearts are the architects of peace,
They mend broken hearts with threads of care,
Weaving a tapestry of genuine embrace.

Caroline 'Ceri' Nazareno-Gabis

Alis Aquilae
(On An Eagle's Wings)

mighty wings in fearless flight
a guardian spirit, fierce and free,
in the realm of azure skies,
where the echo of freedom lies,
cuts through clouds,
in a world anew,
with sharp vision,
a symbol of power, grace, and poise,
above the silence, a victorious voice,
unbound by earth,
a soul unchained,
a beacon of goodwill and inner fire.
a testament to time,
unswayed by fleeting fads and craze,
where the old world ends and the new world lies
your untamed wings, bold and bright,
 giver of dreams, a generous giver,
bless up, a creature of light!

Swapna Behera

Swapna Behera

Swapna Behera is a trilingual poet, translator, environmentalist, editor from India and author of seven books of different genres including one on children's literature on Environment. She is the recipient of International UGADI AWARD 2019, honoured from Gujurat Sahitya Akademi 2022, 2021 International Poesis Award of Honor as Jury, Pentasi B World Fellow Poet, Honoured Poet of India from Seychelles Government and International awards from Algeria, Morocco, Kajhakhstan, modern Arabic Literary Renaissance of Egypt, International Arts Council Argentina etc. Her stories, poems, articles are published in many International and National magazines and ezines. Her poem A NIGHT IN THE REFUGEE CAMP is translated into 67 languages. She has received over 60 National and International Awards. At present she is the Cultural Ambassador for India and South Asia of Inner Child and the life member of Odisha Environmental Society

Email
swapna.behera@gmail.com

Web Site
http://swapnabehera.in/

Tang Dynasty Poet : Li Bai

the romantic poet from China of seventh century
"Drinking alone beneath the moon"
wrote on friendship, solitude
 the passage of time and joys of nature
with brilliant imagination
shade and light are different in every valley
 Li Bai; the epitome of the classic Tang Dynasty
his quiet night thoughts
the cherry blossom party
prolific he was with
clear imagery and conversational tone
the first one to write four hundred sixty-four tourism poetry
 an outstanding tourism master of aesthetics
nature worship is inseparable as influence of Taoism
immortal poet he was who influenced Ezra Pound and
Gustav Mahier
his witty poetry depicts ethics and death
 a translator and illustrious poet of the emperor's court
born in a poor family, married the daughter of the prime
minister
travelled from the Yellow River to the Yangtze River
a Taoist he was
recognized for his clever and inventive poems
certainly, he was a bird
who translated silence

Stop War

stop war at the courtyard
children are playing
mother is worshiping
the fragrance of Tulsi plant filling the air
stop war at the war field
who has allowed you to abuse the vast greenery?
you throw bombs, kill innocent youth
millions of refugees are running in search of a home
the field is red
smokes are here and there
the battle field can grow tons of rice and crops
why do you waste the plasmas and blood cells
 when you can never create a drop of blood
stop war
don't destroy mother nature
don't ever try to fill carbons and toxic poisons in the lungs
war has multiple tentacles
it destroys and the aftermath creates fear
war gives birth to war and again war so on
stop war
the baby is in the womb
it wants to smile
the school is destroyed devastated
human rights are violated
child abuse is increased
women are panicked
the strong and healthy youth are killed in the war
ego, super ego is marching forward
peace seminars are going on
inner peace creates and accommodates volumes of
harmony
love sustains

Swapna Behera

stop war
don't waste the breast milk
love calls you from the womb
death is painful
premature death is still more aching
babies need to smile
can you please sow smiles and love in each battle field?
someone is crying
just stop a while
tears of one are tears of all
tears echo for millions of years
stop war
stop war
I say
stop war

The Loquacious Girl on the Street

she is gob-smacked
the slum girl
peeps through the holes of the wall
of the school boundary
she imagines alphabets, dreams vowels and consonants
her palm is warm
she sings the anthem of plastic democracy
in every rally she marches with her mother
the hired head
 useless metaphors hang and bang every where
slogans are written on each coffin of a martyr
rivers dry and the fishes are fried on every rich man's table
the girl needs a frock to hide her dignity
each night she is barbequed on the screw of hunger
the aftermath of hunger is mysterious
 the garrulous girl losses the speech
to carry her baby
whose father's identity she never knows
life hangs as dry leaves on the electric wire
lust wins and
the vivacious girl bleeds silence forever

Swapna Behera

Albert 'Infinite' Carrasco

Albert 'Infinite' Carassco

Albert "Infinite The Poet" Carrasco is an urban poet, mentor and public speaker.

Albert believes his experience of growing up in poverty, dealing with drugs and witnessing murder over and over were lessons learnt, in order to gain knowledge to teach. Albert's harsh reality and honesty is a powerfully packed punch delivered through rhyme. Infinite grew up in the east part of the Bronx and still resides there, so he knows many young men will follow the same dark path he followed looking for change. The life of crime should never be an option to being poor but it is, very often.

Infinite poetry @lulu.com

Alcarrasco2 on YouTube

Infinite the poet on reverbnation

Infinite Poetry

www.lulu.com/us/en/shop/al-infinite-carrasco/infinite-poetry/paperback/product-21040240.html

www.innerchildpress.com/albert-carrasco

Li Bai (inspired by Bluebird)

I can't let people see me,
I show them persona.
Everyone swears they know me,
I beg to differ.
Alone I'm free,
I'm a solo drifter.
Amongst a crowd…
My exterior gives shelter.
My dancing partners have no idea
that they're dancing with a stranger.
Most of the time I drink to drown my interior,
But it just treads in that dark water.
I guess it has conscious buoyancy.
My writings are painted pictures,
Portraits that depict life, love and laughter,
masking the face of my disaster.
How can I be so popular and so unknown at the same time?
My inebriation is also my attraction,
I drink to pour out artistic expression.
When I'm alone with peace and quiet,
I let myself free to incite a silent riot.

On Stage

When I'm on stage I walk up to the mic and pause for a few seconds as I soak in the scenery. All eyes are on me. I don't have stage fright it's just amazing to me that I'm standing there as an artist preparing to recite what I write. I've always loved the art of storytelling through rhyme but never in a million years would I have thought I'll be up there spitting mine. I guess I had to live it in order to depict concrete jungle imagery clearly. I went through a lot in order to be here, very little sunshine, but lots of rain, joy, but more pain, blood, sweat and a lot of tears. Adrenaline flows, I shuffle pieces in my head and pick a few for the show, I'm so eager to blow that I just go in and let everybody know who I am on the outro. I'm hungry up there, I cook, mix and bust my gun till it's murder 1 up there, I count racks, girl and boy hundred packs and all the funeral cards of those that got sent back up there. The trap is all around me, my words will make you feel as if you was with me in that NYCHA lobby, court room and cemetery.

Street Dreaming

I still blow it, I don't drink often but when I do I pour out a bit for those that R.I.P before I take a sip. Salud my kin. Infinite went from the bricks to cages, from the bricks to stages, from the bricks to pages, been going thru it leveling up makn power moves, ya know boss life phases.

I'm always going to rep my genre hard like a body when it's soul returns to the father... I've always been around gangsters, drugs and guns growing up in a hood where parks were full of chalk marks outlining a murder. The only people out we're hustlers, killers, fiends and undercovers, I walked on shells of all calibers, needles with blood all over, old stems clogged with cut/baking soda and caps of all colors, got caught up young and left my mark like crayola, the block knows what is, bust everything from hands to shoulder stocks and went thru the entire spectrum... Roy G Biv. There's a million ways to die, if ya crossed me in these housing developments you'll be the million and one experiment. Had to stay alive by any means necessary whether it's a jagged edge or a pointy tip you're gonna get done dirty, don't start none won't be none, all I was doing was trying to get out of poverty by stacking my money to get out the slums.

Michelle Joan Barulich

Michelle Joan Barulich

Michelle Joan Barulich was born in Honolulu, Hawaii on the island of Oahu. She started writing poetry and songs with her younger brother Paul. They have written many songs in their teen years. She is currently studying Alternative Medicine and would like to become a Homeopathic Doctor. Michelle loves all kinds of animals and birds; she does wild rehabilitation. She has also rescued rock pigeons that make great pets.

https://www.facebook.com/michelle.barulich

Michelle Joan Barulich

Li Bai

Li Bai was a Chinese poet
He is considered one of the most important poets
Of the Tang dynasty
His poems became models
For celebrating the joys of friendship, nature and solitude
And the joys of drinking
It was said that while some may have drunk more wine
Then Li Bai no one has written more poems about wine
One of his famous poems was called
The moon has never known how to drink
Also, as a skilled calligrapher
It remains in the Palace Museum in Beijing China
Li Bai's poetry have been called
The greatest of all time by the Ming dynasty.

Losers

These bleeding hearts
Die from where they rose
A dead- end town
Where lover's chose
A new way of life
And it's coming too soon
I cannot decide
Nor can I consume
There's just one thing
I'd like to know
There's just one thing
Are we the losers
Are we anyone at all?
Are we the losers
Are we anyone?

Co-writer: Paul Barulich

Michelle Joan Barulich

Inside the Light

Growing up in this world
Was very hard to take
But growing up in the future
Will be much harder to make
I see no doors open for me
Chances are there locked
I see no keys being handed to me
Because the boats in the harbor are docked
Inside the light
Holds nightmares for me
Inside the light
death is all I see
Inside the light I'm reaching in
Where happiness is something, people have to lend
Sitting in silence in my room
I'm reaching the end
Where happiness something people have to pretend.

Co-writer: Paul Barulich

Eliza Segiet

Eliza Segiet

Eliza Segiet graduated with a Master's Degree in Philosophy at Jagiellonian University.

Received *Global Literature Guardian Award* – from Motivational Strips, World Nations Writers Union and Union Hispanomundial De Escritores (UHE) 2018.

Nominated for the Pushcart Prize 2019, 2021.

Laureate *Naji Naaman Literary Prize 2020*,

International Award Paragon of Hope (2020),

World Award 2020 *Cesar Vallejo* for Literary Excellence. Laureate of the Special Jury *Sahitto International Award* 2021, World Award *Premiul Fănuş Neagu* 2021.

Finalist *Golden Aster Book* World Literary Prize 2020, *Mili Dueli* 2022, Voci nel deserto 2022.

At the international Festival of Poetry CAMPIONATO MONDIALE DI POESIA (2021/2022) she won the title of vice-champion of the world.

Award BHARAT RATNA RABINDRANATH TAGORE INTERNATIONAL AWARD (2022).

Award - *World Poets Association* (2023).

Laureate Between words and infinity *"International Literary Award (2023).*

The Scent of Wine
In memory of Li Bai*

His world
was filled with longing.
Accompanied by his own shadow,
which lay down and rose with him,
in the moonlight,
he sought consolation.
Not just when
he reflected on the passing of time,
loneliness, beauty
and emotional anguish,
but always was there help at hand
that would cheer him up.

Solitary feasts were a refuge.
From the standing jugs,
lurked the guilty smell of liquor.
When having been drunk,
it gave him smiles and joy,
it made him forget.
It made
his poems
intertwine with goblets of wine,
with the moon, with his shadow
and with the rhythms of a march,
which
– gave him immortality.

* Li Bai (701-762) - one of the most famous wine drinkers. He often celebrated the joy of drinking. With brilliance and great freshness of imagination, he wrote about loneliness, friendship, transience and joys.

Translated by Dorota Stępińska

Black Drops

She can still see you
her dreamed world
in which
she gave up dreams for love.

And now?
On her cheeks,
like rain
run down
the black drops of ink –
the rain of the soul.

With tears she wanted
to drown out her longings,
but she is unable to lose the memories.
Like a camel with its water,
and so she –
carries the weight of the past.

Translated by Artur Komoter

Memories

In your life

she was just an adventure.

Her memories

fade away slowly,

very slowly.

Now she knows

that you are trying the world out yourself

and as before

you talk only

with condensing time.

Translated by Artur Komoter

William S. Peters Sr.

William S. Peters, Sr.

Bill's writing career spans a period of well over 50 years. Being first Published in 1972, Bill has since went on to Author in excess of 50+ additional Volumes of Poetry, Short Stories, etc., expressing his thoughts on matters of the Heart, Spirit, Consciousness and Humanity. His primary focus is that of Love, Peace and Understanding!

Bill says . . .

I have always likened Life to that of a Garden. So, for me, Life is simply about the Seeds we Sow and Nourish. All things we "Think and Do", will "Be" Cause and eventually manifest itself to being an "Effect" within our own personal "Existences" and "Experiences" . . . whether it be Fruit, Flowers, Weeds or Barren Landscapes! Bill highly regards the Fruits of his Labor and wishes that everyone would thus go on to plant "Lovely" Seeds on "Good Ground" in their own Gardens of Life!

to connect with Bill, he is all things Inner Child

www.iaminnerchild.com

Personal Web Site

www.iamjustbill.com

Lĭ Bái

I have found many a spirit
In the bottom of the bottle
Of all types of wine

The ambrosiatic flavors of life
Lay in await
For my arrival
That I may consume their essence
And make it that of mine own

I am inebriated
For good cause
For words have been
The fruit of my labor,
A noble undertaking
That I have taken to the grave
And thus it has become
My epitaph,
For I Am
Lĭ Bái
The capturer of the light
Of the moon

Every

"Every thing must change
Nothing stays the same"

Every bud which becomes a blossom,
And thus a fragrant flower
Has its appointed time
To wither, die
And be no more

Every dream
Accomplished or not
Can only live
Its own lifetime

Every thing with wings
That flies
Will in time
Fall to the ground
And be no more

Every thing ever built
Will rest in ruin
As time takes its toll

Every breath
Dies and returns
To the ether.
Every heartbeat
Is short-lived

Every thought
In time will be forgotten

William S. Peters, Sr.

Every vision
Is blinded
By the presence
Of another

Every experience
Rests in the tomb
Of memories
Awaiting a possible brief
Resurrection

Every lesson
Is susceptible to drown
In that sea
Of 'forgetfulness'

Every hug
Only has a brief lifespan,
As does every smile,
Every frown

Every word spoken
Mutates into
Something other

Every gesture of kindness
Dies to be able
To live in the heart

Every emotion in life
Can not be sustained

Every touch
Is but a moment

Every life must transition
And cross that Rainbow Bridge

But every love,
Lives on forever

"Don't worry about a thing,
'Cause every little thing gonna be all right."

Selflessness

Like a determined and driven moth
Drawn to the flame
Of the candle,
So am I
Drawn and mesmerized
By that holy and divine
Undefinable thing
That burns deeply
Within me

Before birth
I was aware of
That energy
That I was destined to seek
Even though
I have been distracted
Over the years
By this thing
We claim to be
Life ...
But is it?

I have uncloaked my consciousness,
And my soul stands naked
Before creation
For in truth
I am direly in need
To be embraced once again
By the 'Giver'
Of all things

Yes, I do have a Father,
Who provided the seed,
Yes, I do have a Mother
Who nurtured that seed

In her womb of love,
But there is more,
There is that spark
That lit that candle
Which at times
Softly burns,
At other times rages
Consuming me,
Begging me
To draw unto that
Which as I say again
Is undefinable
By my empirical self

To be selfless
Is the aim,
For I tire
Of the rendered definitions of 'self'
I have gathered
During this journey....
Which is why I am
Like a determined and driven moth
Drawn to the flame
Of the candle,
So am I
Drawn and mesmerized
By that holy and divine
Undefinable thing
That burns deeply
Within me.

Narrative :

It was evening time, and we were sitting on our porch with a citronella oil lamp burning. As they say, supposedly the smell and burning of citronella will repel bugs. However, this rather mature moth began to fly into the open flame time and time again. Sure, moths are helplessly drawn to the light, be it artificial, or that, an open flame that threatens their very mortality. You would think that once its wings felt the extreme heat of the open flame, it would avoid it, but it kept coming back again and again until we finally extinguished the torch. ... question .... are moths willful? Do we possess such abandon in seeking and fulfilling our soul-quest for oneness with the light?

August 2024 Featured Poets

Ibrahim Honjo

Khalice Jade

Irma Kurti

Mennadi Farah

Ibrahim Honjo

Inrahim Honjo

Ibrahim Honjo is a Canadian/Bosnian poet-writer, who writes in Bosnian, and English language. He has worked as an economist, journalist, editor, marketing director, and property manager. He is currently retired and resides in Vancouver, BC.

Honjo is author 24 published books in Bosnian Language, (7 books in English, 3 books bilingually (in English and Bosnian language). In addition, 4 joints' books of poems published with Serbian poets. His poems have been represented in more than 70 world anthologies. Some of Honjo's poems have been translated into 19 languages.

He received several prizes for his poetry.

Inrahim Honjo

Autumn Night In Me

Night butterflies land on my shoulders
stars like fireflies setting their soft light
on my sleepy eyes

autumn is sunny and endlessly colorful
salmon going to hatcheries
clouds are wearily flying from east to west
and from north to south

leaves secretly falling from branches
in the rhythm of the Argentine tango

An evening smell of roasted chestnuts
imprisoned in the nose
and a rush of saliva in the mouth

The voice of an owl
is breaking the silence of the night
in me, everything is sealed
as the greatest secret

some new disquietude ravages my soul
and some new unusual thought
is breaking my soul

the autumn sprinkled my soul
I sigh feeling the beauty of the landscape

Dying In A Poem

No, I'm not dying my darling
It is me being born again
in a poem without enthusiasm and wings
after all cannonades

just keep silent, watch and wait
for me to start crying or smiling
wait for me to see off the last great war, weeping
wait for me to smile to a new life

wait
just wait
for a poem to start speaking inside of me
and let her cry over everything that was
and smile at everything that will come
cuddle her lament
and her laughter on your chest
hug the winged poem
and let her fly with the first strong wind
far, wide, deep and high
and watch
just watch
how I am born frozen in the poem
and how I'm leaving with the poem
after the Great War
to rest from all past and future cannonades

please
do not cry on departure, like you used to
we mourned goodbyes long ago
on the platforms of many cities

Inrahim Honjo

let's smile together
for everything that has passed
and everything that is coming
look around you
and wait for a bird to sing
and cheerfully fly to no return

and I want you to know
everything that comes must leave

and it never comes back

take my hand and hold it firmly
smile at my last trip
it's time for the last goodbye
the devil came to claim his own
he is the only one who comes, goes and returns

Insanity

The beginning of all nonsense is in people
man has nothing to do with it
insanity has no limits
it only has a cradle where it is born and nurtured

from the cradle of insanity
storms and hurricanes are born
earthquakes, rock falls, landslides and wars
insanity is the creator of swords, guns, bombs
and everything that can destroy

insanity is inaugurated in the souls of people
man has nothing to do with it

in vain my poem talks about truth and love
they are on their wobbly feet
and every day they stumble more and more

truth and love are incarcerated
and slowly suppressed
in the way that killers cover their tracks

my poem is alone and powerless to stop it
there is no powerful man to stop the insanity
there is no God almighty
and there's nothing to protect the truth
and love in people

I dread that my poem will become insane
and agree to the eternal darkness of lunatics
I'm scared for man and mankind

I'm dying in disquietude

Inrahim Honjo

Khalice Jade

Khalice Jade

Saliha Ragad, également connue sous le pseudonyme de Khalice Jade, est une artiste polyvalente, écrivaine, peintre, traductrice et ambassadrice internationale de la guérison et de la paix. Malgré des études administratives, son engagement pour la tolérance et la paix est précoce, reconnu dès l'âge de 11 ans. Elle compte à son actif 30 ouvrages personnels, dont des romans, recueils poétiques, essais et contes adaptés au théâtre. À travers ses 11 anthologies pour des causes humanitaires et sa participation à des projets internationaux en faveur de la paix, elle poursuit son combat pour une humanité bienveillante et fraternelle.

♡♡♡

Biography:
Saliha Ragad, also known under the pseudonym Khalice Jade, is a versatile artist, writer, painter, translator, and international ambassador for healing and peace. Despite administrative studies, her commitment to tolerance and peace began early, recognized at the age of 11. She has authored 30 personal works, including novels, poetic collections, essays, and theater-adapted tales. Through her 11 anthologies for humanitarian causes and participation in international peace projects, she continues her fight for a compassionate and fraternal humanity.

Khalice Jade

Les Fils De La Compréhension
Dialogue entre la Poétesse et le Jeune Drogué Alcoolique Nommé Micha :

Poétesse :
--- Au fil des ponts de la compréhension,
Je t'offre une nouvelle direction.
Entre les rives de ton désespoir,
Trouvons un chemin pour te voir renaître.

Micha:
--- Dans l'ombre de ma peine, je suis perdu,
Ces ponts semblent lointains et confus.
Mais si tu dis qu'ils existent vraiment,
Peut-être que je pourrais les trouver, au bout du chemin.

Poétesse :
--- Regarde autour de toi, vois-tu ces lumières,
Guidant ceux qui ont vaincu leurs barrières?
Ce sont des âmes qui ont traversé la nuit,
Pour trouver la paix au-delà de l'oubli.

--- Micha :
Je sens une lueur d'espoir naître en moi,
Peut-être que je pourrais me libérer cette fois.
Tes mots sont comme des étoiles dans la nuit,
Me montrant le chemin vers une vie sans ennui.

Poétesse :
--- Prends ma main, avançons ensemble,
Sur le sentier de la rédemption qui tremble.
Vers la lumière qui brille au loin,
Où les ponts de compréhension nous rejoignent.

Micha :
--- Je suis prêt à affronter ce nouveau départ,
À laisser derrière moi mon ancien état.
Dans cette aventure, nous sommes unis,
Par la force de la compréhension, où règne l'harmonie.

Dans ce dialogue, la Poétesse guide le Jeune Micha vers la guérison et la rédemption grâce au pouvoir des ponts de compréhension.

Khalice Jade

The Threads Of Understanding
Dialogue between the Poetess and the Young Drug Addict Named Micha:

Poetess :
--- Along the bridges of understanding,
I offer you a new direction.
Between the shores of your despair,
Let's find a way to see you reborn.

Micha :
--- In the shadow of my pain, I'm lost,
These bridges seem distant and confused.
But if you say they truly exist,
Maybe I could find them, at the end of the road.

Poetess :
--- Look around you, do you see those lights,
Guiding those who have overcome their barriers?
They are souls who have crossed the night,
To find peace beyond oblivion.

Micha:
--- I feel a glimmer of hope arising within me,
Perhaps I could break free from this time.
Your words are like stars in the night,
Showing me the way to a life without boredom.

Poetess:
--- Take my hand, let's move forward together,
On the trembling path of redemption.
Towards the light shining in the distance,
Where the bridges of understanding join us.

Micha:
--- I'm ready to face this new beginning,
To leave behind my old state.
In this adventure, we are united,
By the power of understanding, where harmony reigns.

In this dialogue, the Poetess guides the Young Micha towards healing and redemption through the power of bridges of understanding.

Khalice Jade

La Ronde De La Paix

Pour la paix, j'écris, je cris je chante et , je danse,
Entre les mots, entre les vers, une symphonie d'espérance.
Cherchant un refuge dans ce monde en transe,
Où chaque mot résonne en une douce cadence.
Sous les cieux étoilés de ma quête,
Je tisse des rêves, des espoirs en fête.
Comme un phénix, je renaîtrai, tête haute,
Bravant les tempêtes, déployant mes ailes, sans faute.
Au fil des strophes, une histoire se dévoile,
Comme une aurore qui éclaire l'ombre du voile.
Le prix de la paix , écrit dans, le sable, dans les étoiles,
Un hymne vibrant, une mélodie qui dévoile.
En poésie, je m'égare, libre et sauvage,
Explorant l'âme, repoussant chaque cage.
Comme le souffle du vent sur une plage,
Je persiste, je rêve, dans ce doux voyage.

Dans l'harmonie des jours à venir,
Les enfants du Monde s'unissent, sans médire.
Une méga ronde, main dans la main,
Ici, là-bas, autour du globe, elle fait son chemin.
Pas de frontières, juste la fraternité,
Une danse de paix, pleine de sincérité.
Autour du monde, elle se déploie,
Comme un doux murmure qui apaise et évoque la joie.

The Dance Of Peace

For peace, I write, I shout, I sing, and I dance,
Between the words, between the verses, a symphony of hope.
Seeking refuge in this world in trance,
Where each word resonates in a sweet cadence.
Under the starry skies of my quest,
I weave dreams, hopes in celebration.
Like a phoenix, I shall rise, head held high,
Braving storms, spreading my wings, no room for denial.
Through the verses, a story unfolds,
Like a dawn illuminating the shadow of the veil.
The price of peace, written in the sand, in the stars,
A vibrant anthem, a melody that reveals.
In poetry, I wander, free and wild,
Exploring the soul, pushing against every cage.
Like the breath of the wind on a beach,
I persist, I dream, in this gentle journey.
In the harmony of days to come,
Children of the World unite, without scorn.
A mega round, hand in hand,
Here, there, around the globe, it finds its way.
No borders, just fraternity,
A dance of peace, full of sincerity.
Around the world, it unfolds,
Like a soft whisper that soothes and evokes joy.

Khalice Jade

Là-Bas...
La Quête des sens

À la lueur des écus, une quête sans mesure,
Pour amasser fortune, une vie en aventure.
Mais or et argent, froids, en leur silence,
N'apaisent point l'âme, ni ne chassent l'absence.

Au banquet de l'existence, où l'argent est convive,
Honneur réel revêt l'amour qui enivre.
Les liens tissés, plus précieux que l'or étincelant,
Forment la trame d'une vie, de jours doux et palpitants.

La table opulente, festin matériel,
N'est qu'un décor éphémère, un jeu superficiel.
L'essence profonde, la richesse véritable,
Résident dans les cœurs, doux et inaltérables.

Écus et billets, froids entre les mains,
Peuvent acheter des biens, mais non le divin.
Car la vraie richesse, douce mélodie du cœur,
Résonne dans l'amour, éternel vainqueur.

Ainsi, ne perdons point l'essentiel en chemin,
Dans l'ivresse des richesses, gardons notre écrin.
Force pour aider, amour pour guider,
La vie prend tout son sens, en douceur partagé.

There...
The Quest for Meaning

In the glow of coins, a quest immeasurable,
To amass fortune, a life so pleasurable.
But gold and silver, cold in their silence,
Do not soothe the soul, nor chase the absence.

At life's banquet, where money is a guest,
True honor lies in love's sweet zest.
The bonds we weave, more precious than gold,
Form the fabric of life, with days warm and bold.

The opulent table, material feast,
Is but a fleeting backdrop, a superficial beast.
True wealth's essence, its domain so real,
Resides in hearts, gentle and ideal.

Coins and bills, cold between hands,
May buy goods, but not the divine lands.
For true wealth, that sweet heart's tune,
Resides in love, eternal boon.

So let us not lose the essential on the way,
In the intoxication of riches, let's keep our array.
Strength to aid, love to guide,
Life finds its meaning in shared deeds.

Khalice Jade

Irma Kurti

Irma Kurti

Irma Kurti is an Albanian poet, writer, lyricist, journalist, and translator and has been writing since she was a child. She is a naturalized Italian and lives in Bergamo, Italy. Kurti has won numerous literary prizes and awards in Albania, Italy, Switzerland, USA, Philippines, Lebanon and China. Irma Kurti has published 28 books in Albanian, 24 in Italian, 15 in English, and two in French. She has also translated 19 books by different authors, and all of her own books into Italian and English. Her books have been translated and published in 15 countries.

Disorientated

Early morning.
My thoughts
wander,
disorientated,
without
knowing yet
what direction
to take.

The sun road
that radiates
colors, light
full of magic
or the alley
of a gray cloud?

Early morning.
Only the echo
of my thoughts
is heard as they
crash with one
another and
rotate as in a
game, trying
to choose
between sun
and shade.

Ice Between My Fingers

I wanted to hear your voice.
My heart would blossom like
a flower; my joy would flow
just like a stream through the
long telephone wire.

I would bring the spring into
my hands, bird songs, a wealth
of buds. I would watch this
scary and chaotic world with
happy and loving eyes.

I wanted to hear your voice
and touch happiness with
my hands, but they feel cold,
so between my fingers
I now have only ice and frost.

We Had The Sea Close By

We had the sea close by; wide and infinite
in its anger, it tried hard to enter our words.
We had the sea close by; it didn't take much
to hold the waves in our hands. Only a step
would be enough, and the particles of sand
between our fingers would have penetrated.

But I had you close to my soul. The noises,
the waves vanished at sunset, a thousand
particles of sand faded, lost somewhere. It
was your voice that remained; like a cradle
it rocked me with the tenderness of a wave.

Mennadi Farah

Mennadi Farah

Mennadi Farah, Algerian engaged poet, my writings aim to spread joy, hope and happiness in the world. I also write for denouncing the violence against children throughout the world by using words touching the consciousness and the soul of the man... the human

Mennadi Farah

Espérance

Si le bonheur était à acheter
Je me l'aurais procuré et j'en aurais fait des dons .

S' il était des fleurs à cultiver
J'aurais récolté le nectar en faisant une boisson .

Si le bonheur était à adorer
Je l'aurais fait prophète de toutes les religions .

Si le bonheur était à aimer
Venus en toi j'aurais été médaillon .

S'il était à admirer
Aphrodite , j'aurais porté tes flans .

Si le bonheur était à féconder
J'aurais été sa femme et mon fils cupidon .

S' il était une terre à peupler
J'aurais uni l'humanité en une seule nation.

Hope

If happiness could be bought
I would have bought it and given it away.

If flowers were to be cultivated
I would have harvested the nectar and made a drink of it.

If happiness was to be worshipped
I would have made him a prophet of all religions .

If happiness were to be loved
Venus in you I would have been a medallion .

If it was to admire
Aphrodite , I would have worn your flans .

If happiness was to be impregnated
I would have been his wife and my son cupid.

If it was a land to populate
I would have united humanity into a single nation.

l'Eveil

Je suis l'éclat du ciel.
Je suis lumière qui courtise la terre,
Dans les cœurs, pointe une nouvelle ère.

Je voltige sur monts et nuages ,
Je saluerai les âmes en quête de repères.
Je me ferai soleil et rechaufferai les cœurs.

Je serai astres et étoiles sans orgueil.
Mon ivresse et ma volée n'ont pas de frontières,
Je hisserai l'emblème de l'humanité entière.

Vers d'autres globes, une prière sans pareille,
Je repartirai les graines de nectaire.
Je serai rayons des galaxies et l'univers.

Mon ascension n'a ni degré ni échelle.
Je serai démon envers Hucifer.
Je serai harmonie qui désarme l'enfer.

Je tisserai les liens et les rendrai ficelles,
Les cieux ouverts aux prières sincères,
Pour une vie nouvelle et prospère.

Awakening

I am the brightness of the sky.
I am light that courts the earth,
In hearts, a new era dawns.

I flutter over mountains and clouds,
I will greet the souls in search of bearings.
I will make myself sun and warm hearts.

I will be stars and stars without pride.
my drunkenness and my flight have no boundaries,
I will raise the emblem of all humanity.

Towards other globes, an unparalleled prayer,
I will leave the nectary seeds again.
I will be rays of galaxies and the universe.

My ascension has neither degree nor scale.
I will be a demon towards Hucifer.
I will be harmony that disarms hell.

I will weave the bonds and make them strings,
The heavens open to sincere prayers,
For a new and prosperous life.

Mennadi Farah

Valeureuse Paix

Celui qui cherche la paix, la veut tout entière.
Ma quiétude n'a besoin ni d'armes ni de fer,
Ni bataillons ou tambours et bruit de tonnerres.
Elle est faite de sentiments nobles et sincères.

La paix n'est ni trêve ni pacte ou amnistie.
Elle se cultive avec tact et modestie.
Elle se répand partout sans contrepartie.
C'est une vertu qui n'a pas de prix.

La paix est dans nos abysses et dans les airs.
Elle n'a ni territoires ni frontières.
On ne peut la délimiter...on l'acquiert,
Sans contrat ou argent mais avec un savoir faire.

Valiant Peace

Who seeks peace wants it all.
My peace needs neither arms nor iron,
Nor battalions or drums and thunder.
It is made up of noble and sincere feelings.

Peace is not a truce, a pact or an amnesty.
It is cultivated with tact and modesty.
It spreads everywhere without quid pro quo.
It is a priceless virtue.

Peace is in our depths and in the air.
It has no territories or borders.
It cannot be delimited... it must be acquired,
Without contracts or money, but with know-how.

Remembering

our fallen soldiers of verse

Janet Perkins Caldwell
February 14, 1959 ~ September 20, 2016

Alan W. Jankowski
16 March 1961 ~ 10 March 2017

The Butterfly Effect

"IS" in effect

Inner Child Press News

Published Books

by

Poetry Posse Members

We are so excited to share and announce a few of the current books, as well as the new and upcoming books of some of our Poetry Posse authors.

On the following pages we present to you ...

Inner Child Press News

Alicja Maria Kuberska
Jackie Davis Allen
Gail Weston Shazor
hülya n. yılmaz
Nizar Sartawi
Elizabeth E. Castillo
Faleeha Hassan
Fahredin Shehu
Kimberly Burnham
Caroline 'Ceri' Nazareno
Eliza Segiet
Teresa E. Gallion
Mutawaf Shaheed
William S. Peters, Sr.

Now Available
www.innerchildpress.com

The Year of the Poet XI ~ August 2024

Now Available
www.innerchildpress.com

Inner Child Press News

Now Available
www.innerchildpress.com

The Year of the Poet XI ~ August 2024

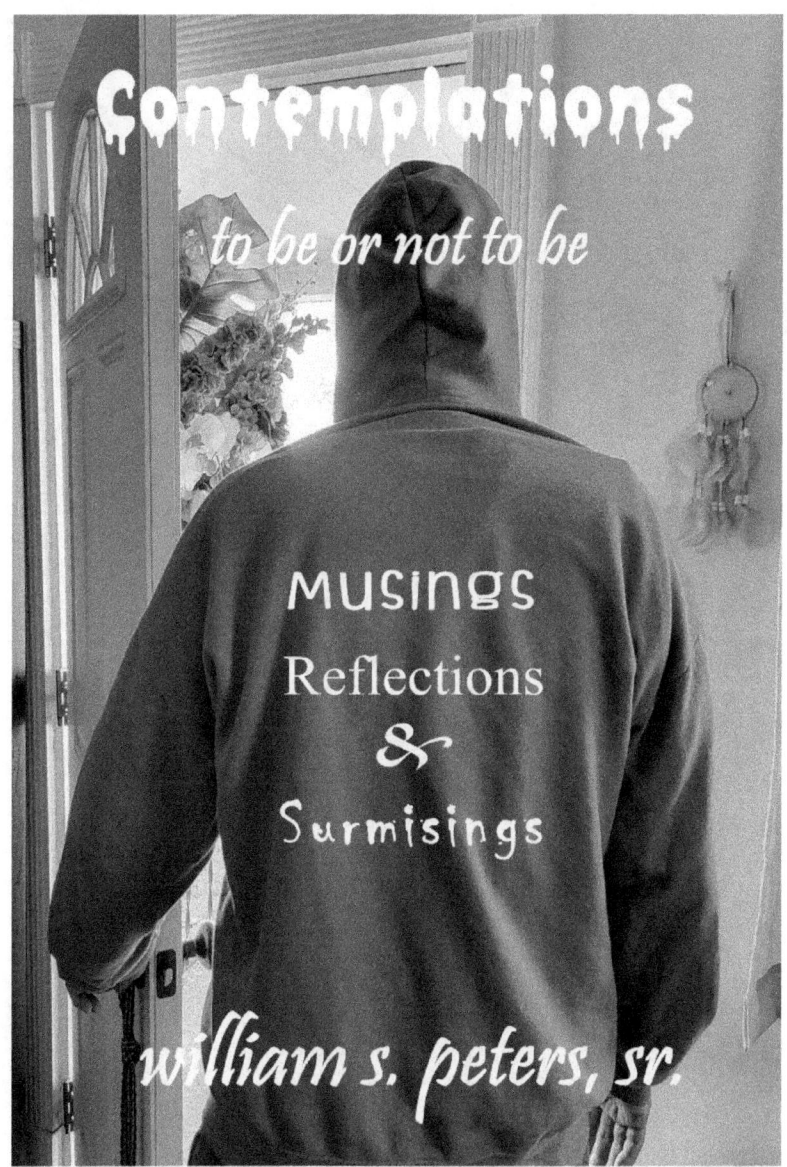

Inner Child Press News

Now Available
www.innerchildpress.com

The Year of the Poet XI ~ August 2024

Now Available
www.innerchildpress.com

Inner Child Press News

Now Available
www.innerchildpress.com

The Year of the Poet XI ~ August 2024

Now Available
www.innerchildpress.com

Inner Child Press News

Now Available
www.innerchildpress.com

The Year of the Poet XI ~ August 2024

Now Available
www.innerchildpress.com

Inner Child Press News

Now Available
www.innerchildpress.com

Inner Child Press News

Now Available at
www.innerchildpress.com

The Year of the Poet XI ~ August 2024

Now Available at
www.amazon.com/gp/product/B08MYL5B7S/ref=
dbs_a_def_rwt_hsch_vapi_tkin_p1_i2

Inner Child Press News

Now Available
www.innerchildpress.com

The Year of the Poet XI ~ August 2024

Now Available
www.innerchildpress.com

Inner Child Press News

Now Available
www.innerchildpress.com

The Year of the Poet XI ~ August 2024

Now Available
www.innerchildpress.com

Now Available
www.innerchildpress.com

The Year of the Poet XI ~ August 2024

The Book of krisar
volume v

william s. peters, sr.

Now Available
www.innerchildpress.com

Inner Child Press News

The Book of krisar

Volume I

william s. peters, sr.

The Book of krisar

Volume II

william s. peters, sr.

Now Available
www.innerchildpress.com

The Year of the Poet XI ~ August 2024

The Book of krisar
Volume III

william s. peters, sr.

The Book of krisar
Volume IV

william s. peters, sr.

Now Available
www.innerchildpress.com

Inner Child Press News

Now Available
www.innerchildpress.com

The Year of the Poet XI ~ August 2024

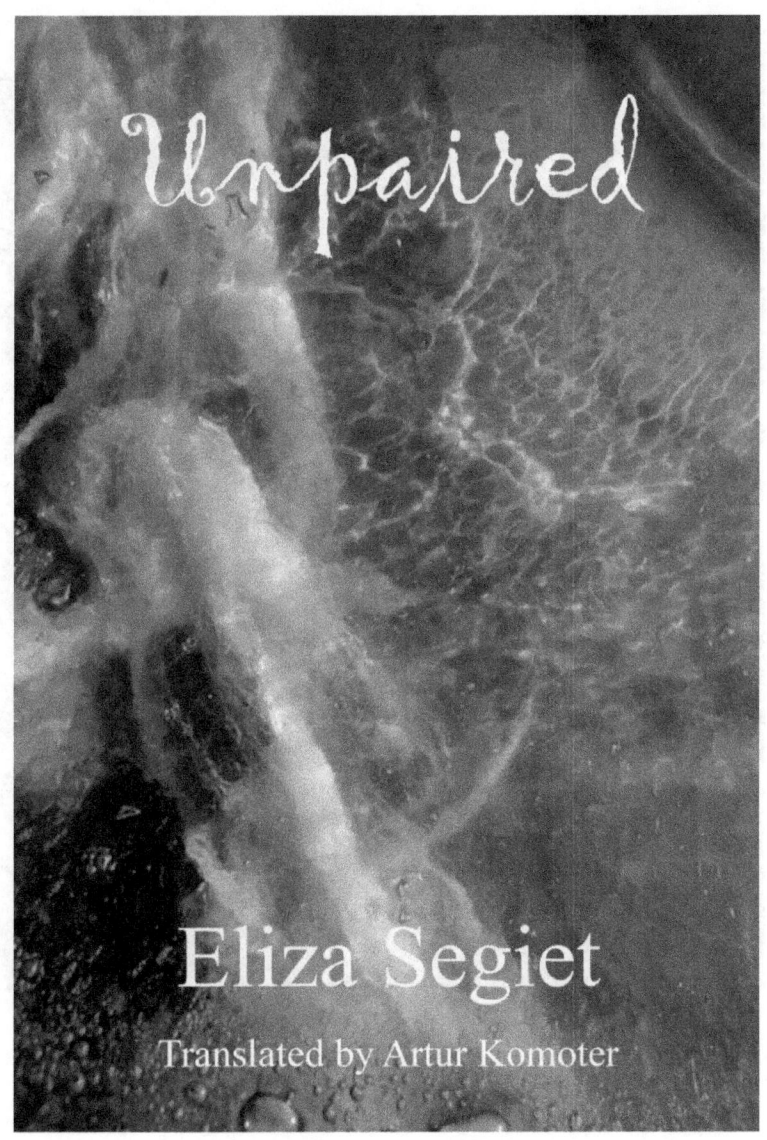

Private Issue
www.innerchildpress.com

Inner Child Press News

Now Available
www.innerchildpress.com

The Year of the Poet XI ~ August 2024

Now Available at
www.innerchildpress.com

Inner Child Press News

Now Available at
www.innerchildpress.com

The Year of the Poet XI ~ August 2024

Now Available at
www.innerchildpress.com

Inner Child Press News

Now Available at
www.innerchildpress.com

The Year of the Poet XI ~ August 2024

HERENOW

FAHREDIN SHEHU

Now Available at
www.innerchildpress.com

Inner Child Press News

Magnetic People

Eliza Segiet

Translated by Artur Komoter

Now Available at
www.innerchildpress.com

The Year of the Poet XI ~ August 2024

Now Available at
www.innerchildpress.com

Inner Child Press News

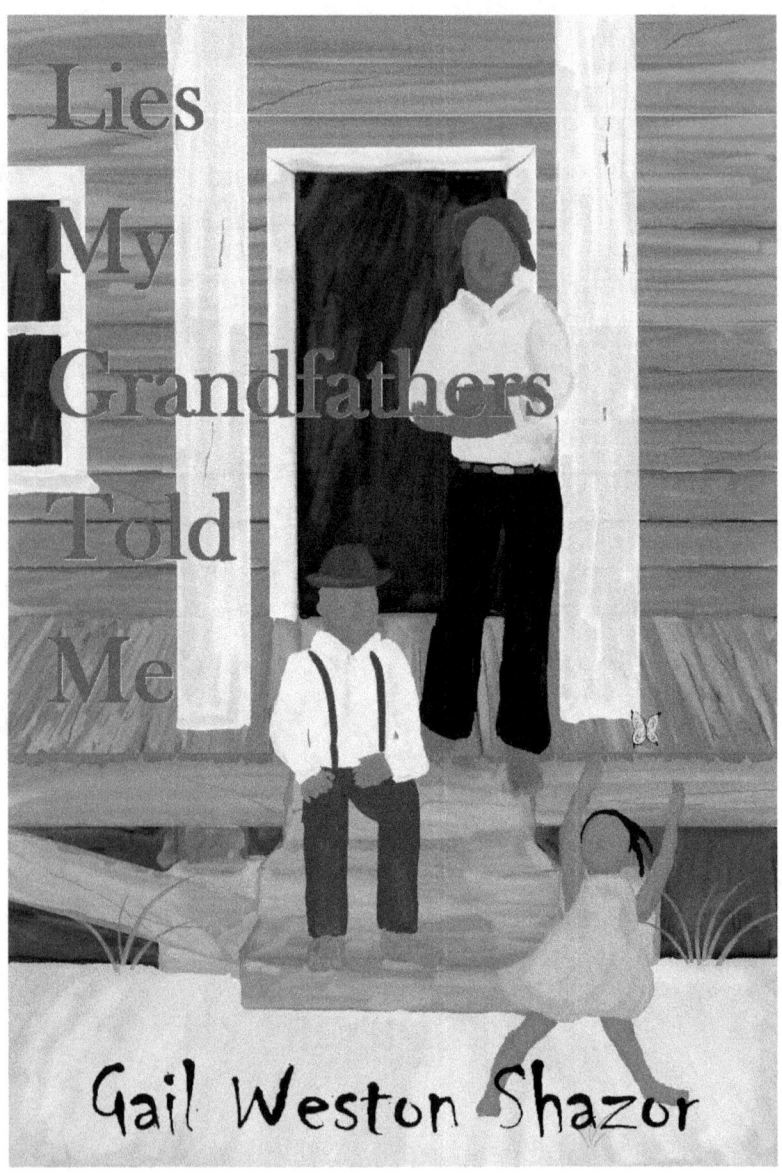

Now Available at
www.innerchildpress.com

The Year of the Poet XI ~ August 2024

Now Available at
www.innerchildpress.com

Inner Child Press News

Now Available at
www.innerchildpress.com

The Year of the Poet XI ~ August 2024

Now Available at
www.innerchildpress.com

Inner Child Press News

Now Available at
www.innerchildpress.com

The Year of the Poet XI ~ August 2024

Now Available at
www.innerchildpress.com

Inner Child Press News

Now Available at
www.innerchildpress.com

The Year of the Poet XI ~ August 2024

Now Available at
www.innerchildpress.com

Inner Child Press News

Now Available
www.innerchildpress.com

Other Anthological works from

Inner Child Press International

www.innerchildpress.com

Inner Child Press Anthologies

Now Available
www.worldhealingworldpeacepoetry.com

Inner Child Press Anthologies

Now Available
www.worldhealingworldpeacepoetry.com

Inner Child Press Anthologies

Now Available
www.worldhealingworldpeacepoetry.com

Inner Child Press Anthologies

Now Available
www.worldhealingworldpeacepoetry.com

Inner Child Press Anthologies

Now Available
www.innerchildpress.com

Inner Child Press Anthologies

Inner Child Press International
&
The Year of the Poet
present

Poetry

the best of 2020

Poets of the World

Now Available
www.innerchildpress.com

Inner Child Press Anthologies

Now Available
www.innerchildpress.com

Inner Child Press Anthologies

Now Available
www.innerchildpress.com

Inner Child Press Anthologies

Now Available
www.innerchildpress.com

Inner Child Press Anthologies

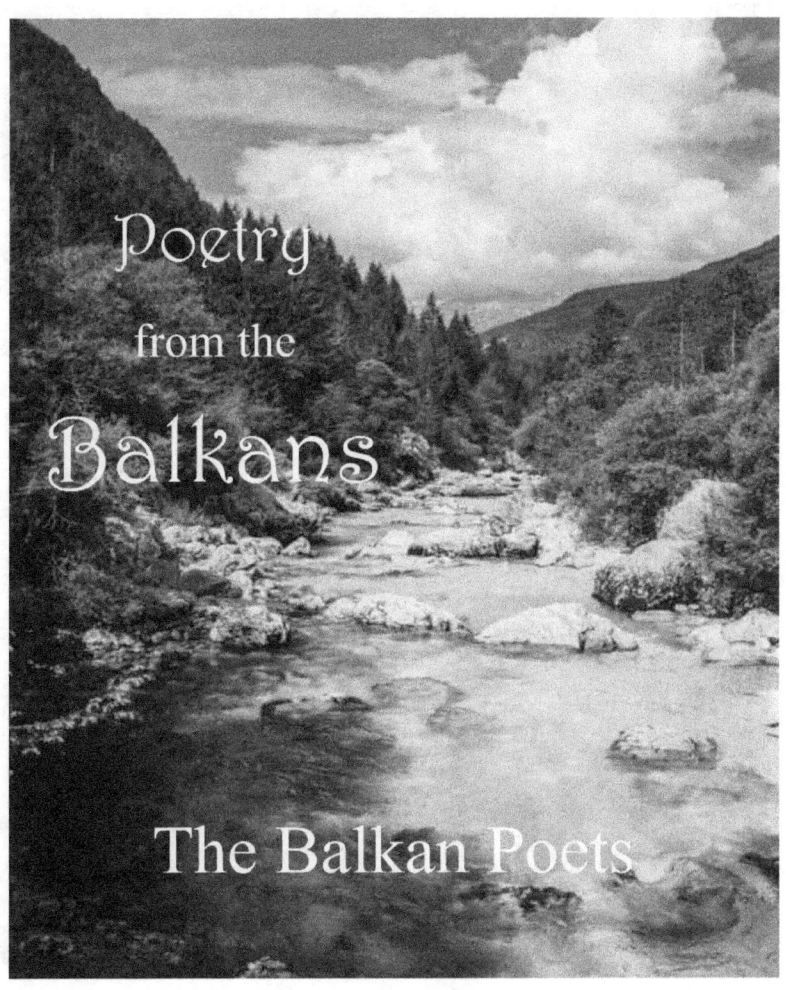

Now Available at
www.innerchildpress.com

Inner Child Press Anthologies

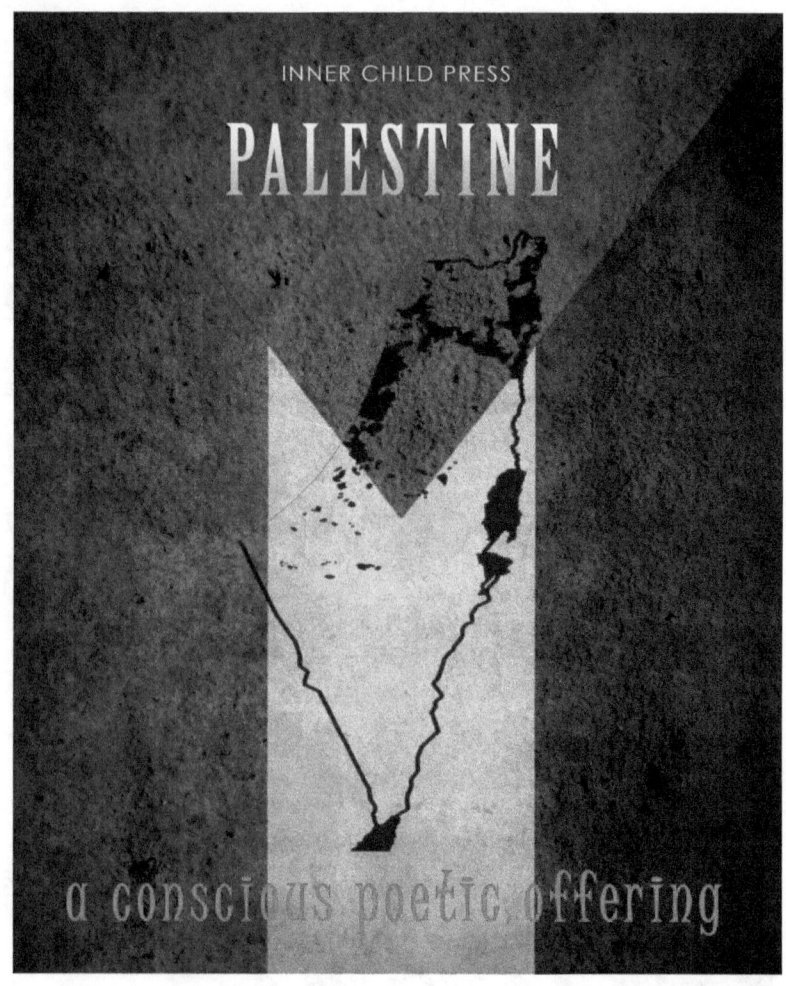

Now Available at
www.innerchildpress.com

Inner Child Press Anthologies

Now Available at
www.innerchildpress.com

Inner Child Press Anthologies

Now Available
www.worldhealingworldpeacepoetry.com

Inner Child Press Anthologies

Now Available
www.worldhealingworldpeacepoetry.com

Inner Child Press Anthologies

Now Available
www.worldhealingworldpeacepoetry.com

Inner Child Press Anthologies

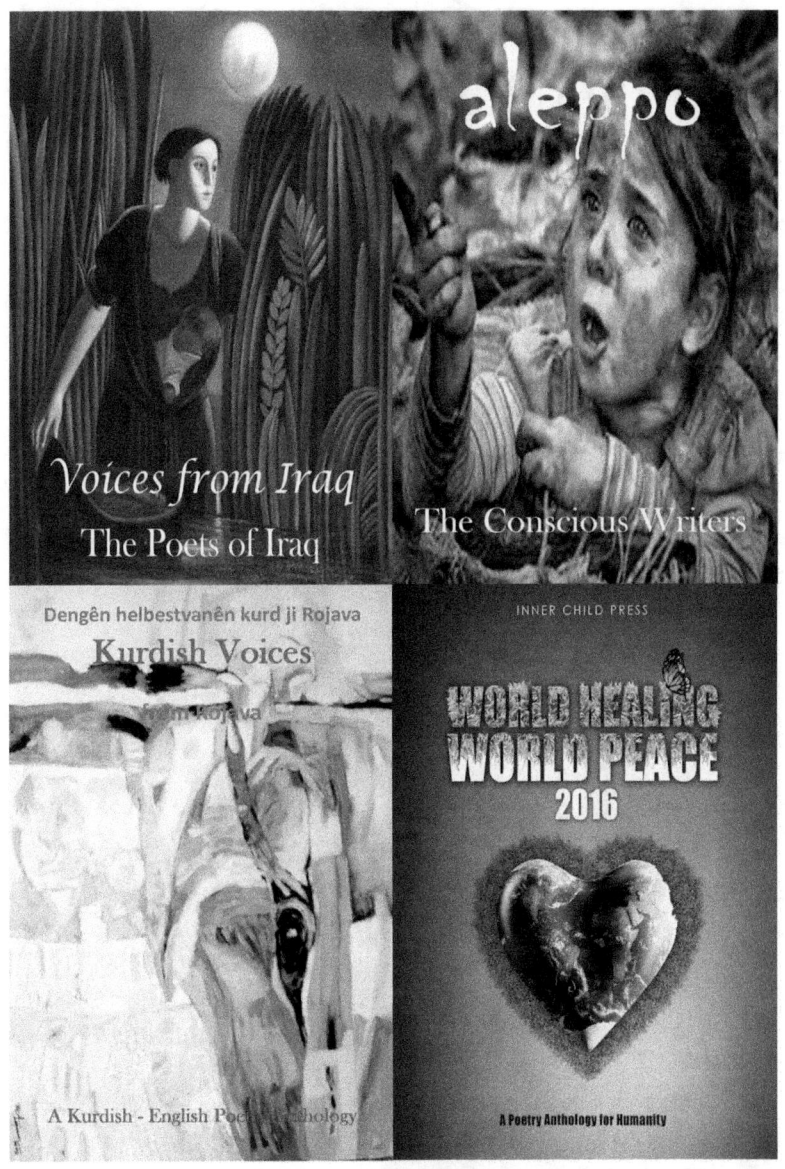

Now Available
www.innerchildpress.com/anthologies

Inner Child Press Anthologies

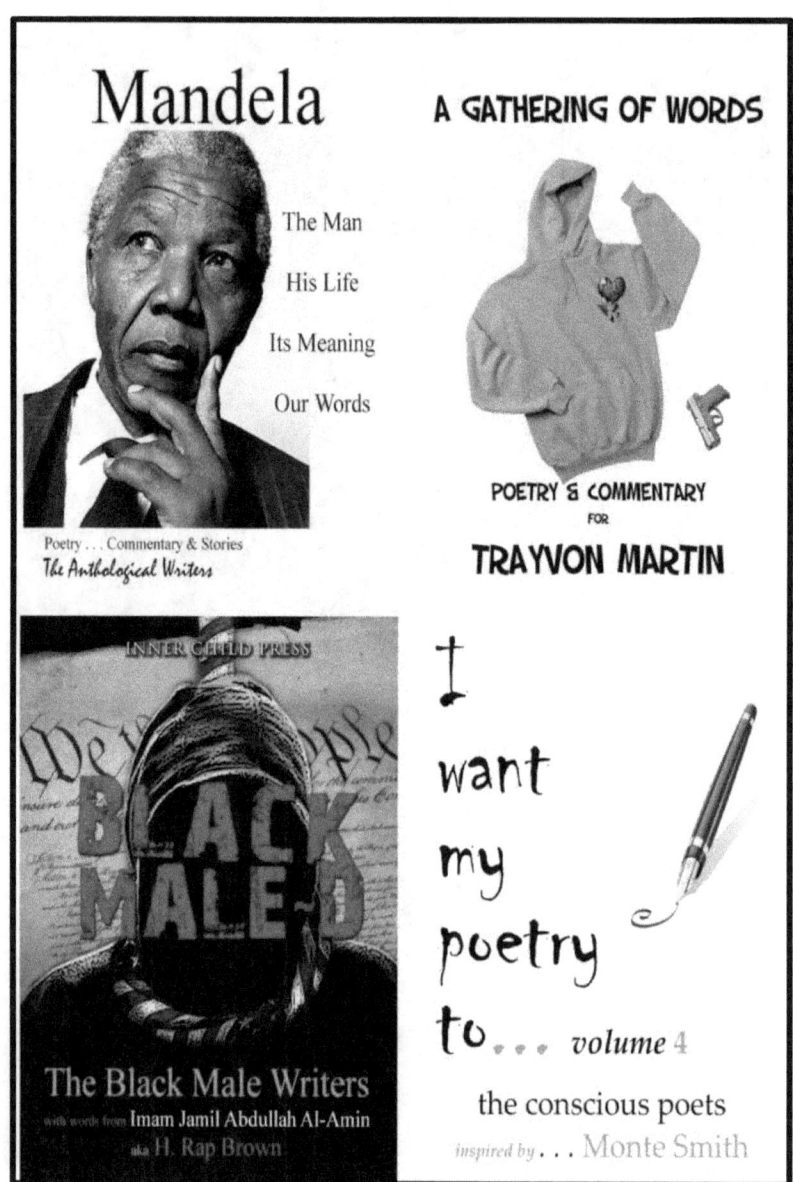

Now Available
www.innerchildpress.com/anthologies

Inner Child Press Anthologies

Now Available
www.innerchildpress.com/anthologies

Inner Child Press Anthologies

Now Available
www.innerchildpress.com/anthologies

Inner Child Press Anthologies

Now Available
www.innerchildpress.com/anthologies

Inner Child Press Anthologies

Now Available
www.innerchildpress.com/the-year-of-the-poet

Inner Child Press Anthologies

Now Available
www.innerchildpress.com/the-year-of-the-poet

Inner Child Press Anthologies

Now Available

www.innerchildpress.com/the-year-of-the-poet

Inner Child Press Anthologies

Now Available
www.innerchildpress.com/the-year-of-the-poet

Inner Child Press Anthologies

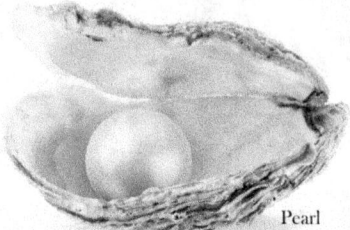

Now Available
www.innerchildpress.com/the-year-of-the-poet

Inner Child Press Anthologies

Now Available
www.innerchildpress.com/the-year-of-the-poet

Inner Child Press Anthologies

Now Available
www.innerchildpress.com/the-year-of-the-poet

Inner Child Press Anthologies

Now Available
www.innerchildpress.com/the-year-of-the-poet

Inner Child Press Anthologies

Now Available
www.innerchildpress.com/the-year-of-the-poet

Inner Child Press Anthologies

Now Available
www.innerchildpress.com/the-year-of-the-poet

Inner Child Press Anthologies

Now Available

www.innerchildpress.com/the-year-of-the-poet

Inner Child Press Anthologies

The Year of the Poet IV
September 2017

Featured Poets
Martina Reisz Newberry
Ameer Nassir
Christine Fulco Neal
Robert Neal

The Elm Tree

The Poetry Posse 2017

Gail Weston Shazor * Caroline Nazareno * Bismay Mohanty
Teresa E. Gallion * Anna Jakubczak Vel Ratty Adalan
Joe DaVerbal Minddancer * Shareef Abdur – Rasheed
Albert Carrasco * Kimberly Burnham * Elizabeth Castillo
Hülya N. Yılmaz * Faleeha Hassan * Jackie Davis Allen
Jen Walls * Nizar Sartawi * William S. Peters, Sr.

The Year of the Poet IV
October 2017

Featured Poets
Ahmed Abu Saleem
Nedal Al-Qaeim
Sadeddin Shahin

The Black Walnut Tree

The Poetry Posse 2017

Gail Weston Shazor * Caroline Nazareno * Bismay Mohanty
Teresa E. Gallion * Anna Jakubczak Vel Ratty Adalan
Joe DaVerbal Minddancer * Shareef Abdur – Rasheed
Albert Carrasco * Kimberly Burnham * Elizabeth Castillo
Hülya N. Yılmaz * Faleeha Hassan * Jackie Davis Allen
Jen Walls * Nizar Sartawi * William S. Peters, Sr.

The Year of the Poet IV
November 2017

Featured Poets
Kay Peters
Alfreda D. Ghee
Gabriella Garofalo
Rosemary Cappello

The Tree of Life

The Poetry Posse 2017

Gail Weston Shazor * Caroline Nazareno * Bismay Mohanty
Teresa E. Gallion * Anna Jakubczak Vel Ratty Adalan
Joe DaVerbal Minddancer * Shareef Abdur – Rasheed
Albert Carrasco * Kimberly Burnham * Elizabeth Castillo
Hülya N. Yılmaz * Faleeha Hassan * Jackie Davis Allen
Jen Walls * Nizar Sartawi * William S. Peters, Sr.

The Year of the Poet IV
December 2017

Featured Poets
Justice Clarke
Mariel M. Pabroa
Kiley Brown

The Fig Tree

The Poetry Posse 2017

Gail Weston Shazor * Caroline Nazareno * Bismay Mohanty
Teresa E. Gallion * Anna Jakubczak Vel Ratty Adalan
Joe DaVerbal Minddancer * Shareef Abdur – Rasheed
Albert Carrasco * Kimberly Burnham * Elizabeth Castillo
Hülya N. Yılmaz * Faleeha Hassan * Jackie Davis Allen
Jen Walls * Nizar Sartawi * William S. Peters, Sr.

Now Available
www.innerchildpress.com/the-year-of-the-poet

Inner Child Press Anthologies

Now Available
www.innerchildpress.com/the-year-of-the-poet

Inner Child Press Anthologies

Now Available
www.innerchildpress.com/the-year-of-the-poet

Inner Child Press Anthologies

Now Available
www.innerchildpress.com/the-year-of-the-poet

Inner Child Press Anthologies

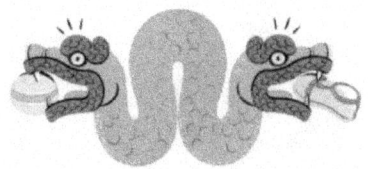

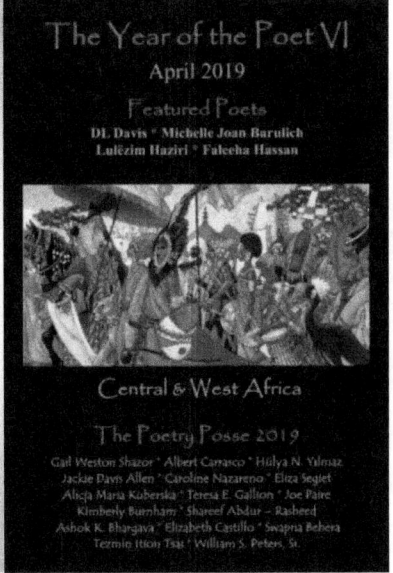

Now Available
www.innerchildpress.com/the-year-of-the-poet

Inner Child Press Anthologies

Now Available
www.innerchildpress.com/the-year-of-the-poet

Inner Child Press Anthologies

Now Available
www.innerchildpress.com/the-year-of-the-poet

Inner Child Press Anthologies

The Year of the Poet VII
January 2020

Featured Poets
B S Tyagi * Ashok Chakravarthy Tholana
Andy Scott * Anwer Ghani

1901 Jean Henry Dunant and Frédéric Passy

The Year of Peace
Celebrating past Nobel Peace Prize Recipients

The Poetry Posse 2020
Gail Weston Shazor * Albert Carasco * Hülya N. Yılmaz
Jackie Davis Allen * Caroline Nazareno * Eliza Segiet
Alicja Maria Kuberska * Teresa E. Gallion * Joe Paire
Kimberly Burnham * Shareef Abdur – Rasheed
Ashok K. Bhargava * Elizabeth Castillo * Swapna Behera
Tezmin Ition Tsai * William S. Peters, Sr.

The Year of the Poet VII
February 2020

Featured Poets
Jennifer Ades * Martina Reisz Newberry
Ibrahim Honjo * Claudia Piccinno

Henri La Fontaine ~ 1913

The Year of Peace
Celebrating past Nobel Peace Prize Recipients

The Poetry Posse 2020
Gail Weston Shazor * Albert Carasco * Hülya N. Yılmaz
Jackie Davis Allen * Caroline Nazareno * Eliza Segiet
Alicja Maria Kuberska * Teresa E. Gallion * Joe Paire
Kimberly Burnham * Shareef Abdur – Rasheed
Ashok K. Bhargava * Elizabeth Castillo * Swapna Behera
Tezmin Ition Tsai * William S. Peters, Sr.

The Year of the Poet VII
March 2020

Featured Poets
Aziz Mountassir * Krishna Paraisa
Hannie Rouweler * Rozalia Aleksandrova

Aristide Briand ~ 1926 ~ Gustav Stresemann

The Year of Peace
Celebrating past Nobel Peace Prize Recipients

The Poetry Posse 2020
Gail Weston Shazor * Albert Carasco * Hülya N. Yılmaz
Jackie Davis Allen * Caroline Nazareno * Eliza Segiet
Alicja Maria Kuberska * Teresa E. Gallion * Joe Paire
Kimberly Burnham * Shareef Abdur – Rasheed
Ashok K. Bhargava * Elizabeth Castillo * Swapna Behera
Tezmin Ition Tsai * William S. Peters, Sr.

The Year of the Poet VII
April 2020

Featured Poets
Rohini Behera * Mircea Dan Duta
Monalisa Dash Dwibedy * NilavroNill Shoovro

Carlos Saavedra Lamas ~ 1936

The Year of Peace
Celebrating past Nobel Peace Prize Recipients

The Poetry Posse 2020
Gail Weston Shazor * Albert Carasco * Hülya N. Yılmaz
Jackie Davis Allen * Caroline Nazareno * Eliza Segiet
Alicja Maria Kuberska * Teresa E. Gallion * Joe Paire
Kimberly Burnham * Shareef Abdur – Rasheed
Ashok K. Bhargava * Elizabeth Castillo * Swapna Behera
Tezmin Ition Tsai * William S. Peters, Sr.

Now Available
www.innerchildpress.com/the-year-of-the-poet

Inner Child Press Anthologies

Now Available
www.innerchildpress.com/the-year-of-the-poet

Inner Child Press Anthologies

Now Available
www.innerchildpress.com/the-year-of-the-poet

Inner Child Press Anthologies

The Year of the Poet VIII
January 2021

Featured Global Poets
Andrew Scott * Debaprasanna Biswas
Shakil Kalam * Changming Yuan

Banksy's The Girl with the Pierced Eardrum

Poetry ... Ekphrasticly Speaking
The Poetry Posse 2020

Gail Weston Shazor * Albert Carasco * Hülya N. Yılmaz
Jackie Davis Allen * Caroline Nazareno * Eliza Segiet
Alicja Maria Kuberska * Teresa E. Gallion * Joe Paire
Kimberly Burnham * Shareef Abdur – Rasheed
Ashok K. Bhargava * Elizabeth Castillo * Swapna Behera
Tezmin Ition Tsai * William S. Peters, Sr.

The Year of the Poet VIII
February 2021

Featured Global Poets
T. Ramesh Babu * Ruchida Barman
Neptune Barman * Faleeha Hassan

Emory Douglas : 1968 Olympics mural

Poetry ... Ekphrasticly Speaking
The Poetry Posse 2021

Gail Weston Shazor * Albert Carasco * Hülya N. Yılmaz
Jackie Davis Allen * Caroline Nazareno * Eliza Segiet
Alicja Maria Kuberska * Teresa E. Gallion * Joe Paire
Kimberly Burnham * Shareef Abdur – Rasheed
Ashok K. Bhargava * Elizabeth Castillo * Swapna Behera
Tezmin Ition Tsai * William S. Peters, Sr.

The Year of the Poet VIII
March 2021

Featured Global Poets
Claudia Piccinno * Mohammed Jabr
Luzviminda Rivera * Nigar Arif

Tatyana Fazlalizadeh

Poetry ... Ekphrasticly Speaking
The Poetry Posse 2021

Gail Weston Shazor * Albert Carasco * Hülya N. Yılmaz
Jackie Davis Allen * Caroline Nazareno * Eliza Segiet
Alicja Maria Kuberska * Teresa E. Gallion * Joe Paire
Kimberly Burnham * Shareef Abdur – Rasheed
Ashok K. Bhargava * Elizabeth Castillo * Swapna Behera
Tezmin Ition Tsai * William S. Peters, Sr.

The Year of the Poet VIII
April 2021

Featured Global Poets
Katarzyna Brus-Sawczuk * Anwesha Paul
Rozalia Aleksandrova * Shahid Abbas

Pablo O'Higgins

Poetry ... Ekphrasticly Speaking
The Poetry Posse 2021

Gail Weston Shazor * Albert Carasco * Hülya N. Yılmaz
Jackie Davis Allen * Caroline Nazareno * Eliza Segiet
Alicja Maria Kuberska * Teresa E. Gallion * Joe Paire
Kimberly Burnham * Shareef Abdur – Rasheed
Ashok K. Bhargava * Elizabeth Castillo * Swapna Behera
Tezmin Ition Tsai * William S. Peters, Sr.

Now Available

www.innerchildpress.com/the-year-of-the-poet

Inner Child Press Anthologies

The Year of the Poet VIII
May 2021

Featured Global Poets
Paramita Mukherjee Mullick * Rose Zerguine
Jaydeep Sarangi * Bismay Mohanty

Diego Rivera

Poetry ... Ekphrasticly Speaking

The Poetry Posse 2021

Gail Weston Shazor * Albert Carasco * Hülya N. Yılmaz
Jackie Davis Allen * Caroline Nazareno * Eliza Segiet
Alicja Maria Kubeska * Teresa E. Gallion * Joe Paire
Kimberly Burnham * Shareef Abdur – Rasheed
Ashok K. Bhargava * Elizabeth Castillo * Swapna Behera
Tezmin Ition Tsai * William S. Peters, Sr.

The Year of the Poet VIII
June 2021

Featured Global Poets
Alonzo "zO" Gross * Lali Tsipi Michaeli
Tareq al Karmy * Tirthendu Ganguly

Rayen Kang

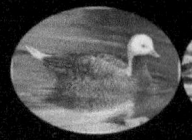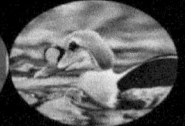

Poetry ... Ekphrasticly Speaking

The Poetry Posse 2021

Gail Weston Shazor * Albert Carasco * Hülya N. Yılmaz
Jackie Davis Allen * Caroline Nazareno * Eliza Segiet
Alicja Maria Kubeska * Teresa E. Gallion * Joe Paire
Kimberly Burnham * Shareef Abdur – Rasheed
Ashok K. Bhargava * Elizabeth Castillo * Swapna Behera
Tezmin Ition Tsai * William S. Peters, Sr.

The Year of the Poet VIII
July 2021

Featured Global Poets
Iram Jaan * Vesna Mundishevska-Veljanovska
Ngozi Olivia Osuoha * Lan Qyqalla

Goncalao Mabunda

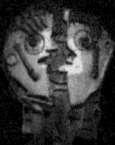

Poetry ... Ekphrasticly Speaking

The Poetry Posse 2021

Gail Weston Shazor * Albert Carasco * Hülya N. Yılmaz
Jackie Davis Allen * Caroline Nazareno * Eliza Segiet
Alicja Maria Kubeska * Teresa E. Gallion * Joe Paire
Kimberly Burnham * Shareef Abdur – Rasheed
Ashok K. Bhargava * Elizabeth Castillo * Swapna Behera
Tezmin Ition Tsai * William S. Peters, Sr.

The Year of the Poet VIII
August 2021

Featured Global Poets
Caroline Laurent Turunc * Kamal Dhungana
Pankhuri Sinha * Paramita Mukherjee Mullick

Mundara Koorang

Poetry ... Ekphrasticly Speaking

The Poetry Posse 2021

Gail Weston Shazor * Albert Carasco * Hülya N. Yılmaz
Jackie Davis Allen * Caroline Nazareno * Eliza Segiet
Alicja Maria Kubeska * Teresa E. Gallion * Joe Paire
Kimberly Burnham * Shareef Abdur – Rasheed
Ashok K. Bhargava * Elizabeth Castillo * Swapna Behera
Tezmin Ition Tsai * William S. Peters, Sr.

Now Available
www.innerchildpress.com/the-year-of-the-poet

Inner Child Press Anthologies

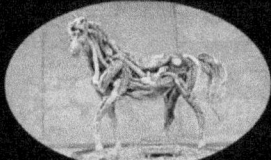

Now Available
www.innerchildpress.com/the-year-of-the-poet

Inner Child Press Anthologies

The Year of the Poet IX
January 2022

Featured Global Poets
**Ratan Ghosh * Christine Neil-Wright
Andrew Scott * Ashok Kumar**

Climate Change : The Ice Cap

Poetry . . . Ekphrasticly Speaking

The Poetry Posse 2021

Gail Weston Shazor * Albert Carasco * Hülya N. Yılmaz
Jackie Davis Allen * Caroline Nazareno * Eliza Segiet
Alicja Maria Kuberska * Teresa E. Gallion * Joe Paire
Kimberly Burnham * Shareef Abdur – Rasheed
Ashok K. Bhargava * Elizabeth Castillo * Swapna Behera
Tezmin Ition Tsai * William S. Peters, Sr.

The Year of the Poet IX
February 2022

Featured Global Poets
Roza Boyanova * Ramón de Jesús Núñez Duval
Mammad Ismayil * Tarana Turan Rahimli

Climate Change and Mountains

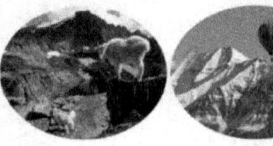

Poetry . . . Ekphrasticly Speaking

The Poetry Posse 2021

Gail Weston Shazor * Albert Carasco * Hülya N. Yılmaz
Jackie Davis Allen * Caroline Nazareno * Eliza Segiet
Alicja Maria Kuberska * Teresa E. Gallion * Joe Paire
Kimberly Burnham * Shareef Abdur – Rasheed
Ashok K. Bhargava * Elizabeth Castillo * Swapna Behera
Tezmin Ition Tsai * William S. Peters, Sr.

The Year of the Poet IX
March 2022

Featured Global Poets
Dimitris P. Kraniotis * Marlene Pasini
Kennedy Ochieng * Swayam Prashant

Climate Change and Space Debris

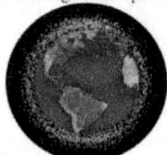

Poetry . . . Ekphrasticly Speaking

The Poetry Posse 2021

Gail Weston Shazor * Albert Carasco * Hülya N. Yılmaz
Jackie Davis Allen * Caroline Nazareno * Eliza Segiet
Alicja Maria Kuberska * Teresa E. Gallion * Joe Paire
Kimberly Burnham * Shareef Abdur – Rasheed
Ashok K. Bhargava * Elizabeth Castillo * Swapna Behera
Tezmin Ition Tsai * William S. Peters, Sr.

The Year of the Poet IX
April 2022

Featured Global Poets
**Alonzo Gross * Dr. Debaprasanna Biswas
Monsif Beroual * Carol Aronoff**

Climate Change and Oceans

Celebrating our 100th Edition

Poetry . . . Ekphrasticly Speaking

The Poetry Posse 2021

Gail Weston Shazor * Albert Carasco * Hülya N. Yılmaz
Jackie Davis Allen * Caroline Nazareno * Eliza Segiet
Alicja Maria Kuberska * Teresa E. Gallion * Joe Paire
Kimberly Burnham * Shareef Abdur – Rasheed
Ashok K. Bhargava * Elizabeth Castillo * Swapna Behera
Tezmin Ition Tsai * William S. Peters, Sr.

Now Available
www.innerchildpress.com/the-year-of-the-poet

Inner Child Press Anthologies

The Year of the Poet IX
May 2022

Featured Global Poets
Ndaba Sibanda * Smrutiranjan Mohanty
Ajanta Paul * Monalisa Dash Dwibedy

Climate Change and Birds

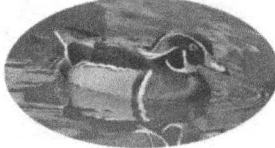

Poetry . . . Ekphrasticly Speaking

The Poetry Posse 2021

Gail Weston Shazor * Albert Carasco * Hülya N. Yılmaz
Jackie Davis Allen * Caroline Nazareno * Eliza Segiet
Alicja Maria Kubeska * Teresa E. Gallion * Joe Paire
Kimberly Burnham * Shareef Abdur – Rasheed
Ashok K. Bhargava * Elizabeth Castillo * Swapna Behera
Tezmin Ition Tsai * William S. Peters, Sr.

The Year of the Poet IX
June 2022

Featured Global Poets
Yuan Changming * Azeezat Okunlola
Tanja Ajtić * Philip Chijioke Abonyi

Climate Change and Trees

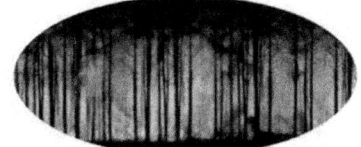

Poetry . . . Ekphrasticly Speaking

The Poetry Posse 2022

Gail Weston Shazor * Albert Carasco * Hülya N. Yılmaz
Jackie Davis Allen * Caroline Nazareno * Eliza Segiet
Alicja Maria Kubeska * Teresa E. Gallion * Joe Paire
Kimberly Burnham * Shareef Abdur – Rasheed
Ashok K. Bhargava * Elizabeth Castillo * Swapna Behera
Tezmin Ition Tsai * William S. Peters, Sr.

The Year of the Poet IX
July 2022

Featured Global Poets
Michelle Joan Barulich * Mili Das
Anna Ferriero * Ujjal Mandal

Climate Change and Animals

Poetry . . . Ekphrasticly Speaking

The Poetry Posse 2022

Gail Weston Shazor * Albert Carasco * Hülya N. Yılmaz
Jackie Davis Allen * Caroline Nazareno * Eliza Segiet
Alicja Maria Kubeska * Teresa E. Gallion * Joe Paire
Kimberly Burnham * Shareef Abdur – Rasheed
Ashok K. Bhargava * Elizabeth Castillo * Swapna Behera
Tezmin Ition Tsai * William S. Peters, Sr.

The Year of the Poet IX
August 2022

Featured Global Poets
Pankhuri Sinha * Abdulloh Abdumominov
Caroline Turunç * Tali Cohen Shabtai

Climate Change and Agriculture

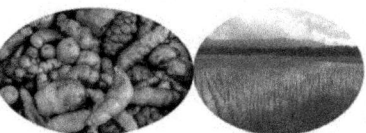

Poetry . . . Ekphrasticly Speaking

The Poetry Posse 2022

Gail Weston Shazor * Albert Carasco * Hülya N. Yılmaz
Jackie Davis Allen * Caroline Nazareno * Eliza Segiet
Alicja Maria Kubeska * Teresa E. Gallion * Joe Paire
Kimberly Burnham * Shareef Abdur – Rasheed
Ashok K. Bhargava * Elizabeth Castillo * Swapna Behera
Tezmin Ition Tsai * William S. Peters, Sr.

Now Available
www.innerchildpress.com/the-year-of-the-poet

Inner Child Press Anthologies

The Year of the Poet IX
September 2022

Featured Global Poets
Ngozi Olivia Osuoha * Biswajit Mishra
Sylwia K. Malinowska * Sajid Hussein

Climate Change and Wind and Weather Patterns

Poetry . . . Ekphrasticly Speaking

The Poetry Posse 2022

Gail Weston Shazor * Albert Carasso * Hülya N. Yılmaz
Jackie Davis Allen * Caroline Nazareno * Eliza Segiet
Alicja Maria Kuberska * Teresa E. Gallion * Joe Paire
Kimberly Burnham * Shareef Abdur – Rasheed
Ashok K. Bhargava * Elizabeth Castillo * Swapna Behera
Tezmin Ition Tsai * William S. Peters, Sr.

The Year of the Poet IX
October 2022

Featured Global Poets
Andrew Kouroupos * Brenda Mohammed
Carthornia Kouroupos * Faleeha Hassan

Climate Change and Oil and Power

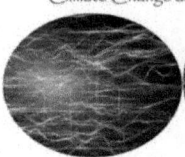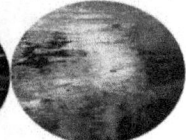

Poetry . . . Ekphrasticly Speaking

The Poetry Posse 2022

Gail Weston Shazor * Albert Carasso * Hülya N. Yılmaz
Jackie Davis Allen * Caroline Nazareno * Eliza Segiet
Alicja Maria Kuberska * Teresa E. Gallion * Joe Paire
Kimberly Burnham * Shareef Abdur – Rasheed
Ashok K. Bhargava * Elizabeth Castillo * Swapna Behera
Tezmin Ition Tsai * William S. Peters, Sr.

The Year of the Poet IX
November 2022

Featured Global Poets
Hema Ravi * Shafkat Aziz Hajam
Selma Kopic * Ibrahim Honjo

Climate Change : Time to Act

Poetry . . . Ekphrasticly Speaking

The Poetry Posse 2022

Gail Weston Shazor * Albert Carasso * Hülya N. Yılmaz
Jackie Davis Allen * Caroline Nazareno * Eliza Segiet
Alicja Maria Kuberska * Teresa E. Gallion * Joe Paire
Kimberly Burnham * Shareef Abdur – Rasheed
Ashok K. Bhargava * Elizabeth Castillo * Swapna Behera
Tezmin Ition Tsai * William S. Peters, Sr.

The Year of the Poet IX
December 2022

Featured Global Poets
Elarbi Abdelfattah * Lorraine Cragg
Neha Bhandarkar * Robert Gibbons

Climate Change Bees, Butterflies and Insect Life

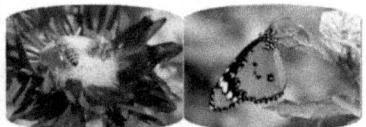

Poetry . . . Ekphrasticly Speaking

The Poetry Posse 2022

Gail Weston Shazor * Albert Carasso * Hülya N. Yılmaz
Jackie Davis Allen * Caroline Nazareno * Eliza Segiet
Alicja Maria Kuberska * Teresa E. Gallion * Joe Paire
Kimberly Burnham * Shareef Abdur – Rasheed
Ashok K. Bhargava * Elizabeth Castillo * Swapna Behera
Tezmin Ition Tsai * William S. Peters, Sr.

Now Available
www.innerchildpress.com/the-year-of-the-poet

Inner Child Press Anthologies

Now Available
www.innerchildpress.com/the-year-of-the-poet

Inner Child Press Anthologies

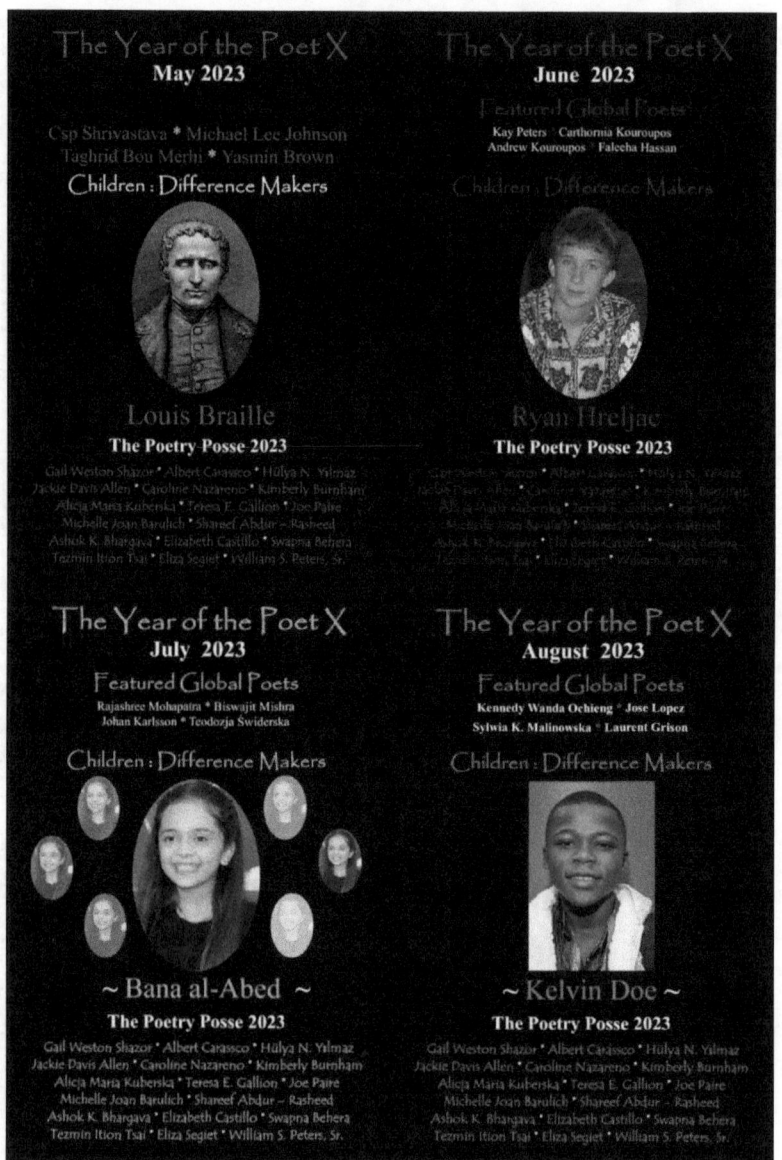

Now Available

www.innerchildpress.com/the-year-of-the-poet

Inner Child Press Anthologies

The Year of the Poet X
September 2023

Featured Global Poets
Eftichia Karpadeli * Chinh Nguyen
Nigar Agalarova * Carmela Cueva

Children : Difference Makers

~ Easton LaChappelle ~

The Poetry Posse 2023
Gail Weston Shazor * Albert Carasco * Hülya N. Yilmaz
Jackie Davis Allen * Caroline Nazareno * Kimberly Burnham
Alicja Maria Kuberska * Teresa E. Gallion * Joe Paire
Michelle Joan Barulich * Shareef Abdur – Rasheed
Ashok K. Bhargava * Elizabeth Castillo * Swapna Behera
Tezmin Ition Tsai * Eliza Segiet * William S. Peters, Sr.

The Year of the Poet X
October 2023

Featured Global Poets
CSP Shrivastava * Huniie Parker
Noreen Snyder * Ramkrishna Paul

Children : Difference Makers

~ Malala Yousafzai ~

The Poetry Posse 2023
Gail Weston Shazor * Albert Carasco * Hülya N. Yilmaz
Jackie Davis Allen * Caroline Nazareno * Kimberly Burnham
Alicja Maria Kuberska * Teresa E. Gallion * Joe Paire
Michelle Joan Barulich * Shareef Abdur – Rasheed
Ashok K. Bhargava * Elizabeth Castillo * Swapna Behera
Tezmin Ition Tsai * Eliza Segiet * William S. Peters, Sr.

The Year of the Poet X
November 2023

Featured Global Poets
Ibrahim Honjo * Balachandran Nair
Xanthi Hondrou-Hil * Francesco Favetta

Children : Difference Makers

~ Jean-Michel Basquiat ~

The Poetry Posse 2023
Gail Weston Shazor * Albert Carasco * Hülya N. Yilmaz
Jackie Davis Allen * Caroline Nazareno * Kimberly Burnham
Alicja Maria Kuberska * Teresa E. Gallion * Joe Paire
Michelle Joan Barulich * Shareef Abdur – Rasheed
Ashok K. Bhargava * Elizabeth Castillo * Swapna Behera
Tezmin Ition Tsai * Eliza Segiet * William S. Peters, Sr.

The Year of the Poet X
December 2023

Featured Global Poets
Caroline Laurent Turunc * Neha Bhandarkar
Shafkat Aziz Hajam * Elarbi Abdelfattah

Children : Difference Makers

~ Melati and Isabel Wijsen ~

The Poetry Posse 2023
Gail Weston Shazor * Albert Carasco * Hülya N. Yilmaz
Jackie Davis Allen * Caroline Nazareno * Kimberly Burnham
Alicja Maria Kuberska * Teresa E. Gallion * Joe Paire
Michelle Joan Barulich * Shareef Abdur – Rasheed
Ashok K. Bhargava * Elizabeth Castillo * Swapna Behera
Tezmin Ition Tsai * Eliza Segiet * William S. Peters, Sr.

Now Available
www.innerchildpress.com/the-year-of-the-poet

Inner Child Press Anthologies

The Year of the Poet XI
January 2024

Featured Global Poets
Til Kumari Sharma * Shafkat Aziz Hajam
Daniela Marian * Eleni Vassiliou – Asteroskon

Renowned Poets

~ Phyllis Wheatley ~
The Poetry Posse 2024

Gail Weston Shazor * Albert Carasso * Hülya N. Yılmaz
Jackie Davis Allen * Caroline Nazareno * Mutawaf Shaheed
Alicja Maria Kuberska * Teresa E. Gallion * Noreen Snyder
Michelle Joan Barulich * Shareef Abdur – Rasheed
Ashok K. Bhargava * Elizabeth Castillo * Swapna Behera
Tezmin Ition Tsai * Eliza Segiet * William S. Peters, Sr.

The Year of the Poet XI
February 2024

Featured Global Poets
Caroline Laurent Turunç * Julio Pavanetti
Lidia Chiarelli * Lina Buividavičiūtė

Renowned Poets

~ Omar Khayyam ~
The Poetry Posse 2024

Gail Weston Shazor * Albert Carasso * Hülya N. Yılmaz
Jackie Davis Allen * Caroline Nazareno * Mutawaf Shaheed
Alicja Maria Kuberska * Teresa E. Gallion * Noreen Snyder
Michelle Joan Barulich * Shareef Abdur – Rasheed
Ashok K. Bhargava * Elizabeth Castillo * Swapna Behera
Tezmin Ition Tsai * Eliza Segiet * William S. Peters, Sr.

The Year of the Poet XI
March 2024

Featured Global Poets
Francesco Favetta * Jagjit Singh Zandu
Carmela Núñez Yukimura Peruana * Michael Lee Johnson

Renowned Poets

~ Nâzim Hikmet ~
The Poetry Posse 2024

Gail Weston Shazor * Albert Carasso * Hülya N. Yılmaz
Jackie Davis Allen * Caroline Nazareno * Mutawaf Shaheed
Alicja Maria Kuberska * Teresa E. Gallion * Noreen Snyder
Michelle Joan Barulich * Shareef Abdur – Rasheed
Ashok K. Bhargava * Elizabeth Castillo * Swapna Behera
Tezmin Ition Tsai * Eliza Segiet * William S. Peters, Sr.

The Year of the Poet XI
April 2024

Featured Global Poets
Hassanal Abdullah * Johny Takkedasila
Rajashree Mohapatra * Shirley Smothers

Renowned Poets

~ William Butler Yeats ~
The Poetry Posse 2024

Gail Weston Shazor * Albert Carasso * Hülya N. Yılmaz
Jackie Davis Allen * Caroline Nazareno * Mutawaf Shaheed
Alicja Maria Kuberska * Teresa E. Gallion * Noreen Snyder
Michelle Joan Barulich * Shareef Abdur – Rasheed
Ashok K. Bhargava * Elizabeth Castillo * Swapna Behera
Tezmin Ition Tsai * Eliza Segiet * William S. Peters, Sr.

Now Available
www.innerchildpress.com/the-year-of-the-poet

Inner Child Press Anthologies

The Year of the Poet XI
May 2024

Featured Global Poets
Binod Dawadi * Petros Kyriakou Veloudas
Rayees Ahmad Kumar * Solomon C Jatta

Renowned Poets

~ Makhanlal Chaturvedi ~

The Poetry Posse 2024
Gail Weston Shazor * Albert Carasco * Hülya N. Yılmaz
Jackie Davis Allen * Caroline Nazareno * Mutawaf Shaheed
Alicja Maria Kuberska * Teresa E. Gallion * Noreen Snyder
Michelle Joan Barulich * Shareef Abdur – Rasheed
Ashok K. Bhargava * Elizabeth Castillo * Swapna Behera
Tezmin Ition Tsai * Eliza Segiet * William S. Peters, Sr.

The Year of the Poet XI
June 2024

Featured Global Poets
C. S. P Shrivastava * Maria Evelyn Quilla Soleta
Moulay Cherif Chebihi Hassani * Swayam Prashant

Renowned Poets

~ Langston Hughs ~

The Poetry Posse 2024
Gail Weston Shazor * Albert Carasco * Hülya N. Yılmaz
Jackie Davis Allen * Caroline Nazareno * Mutawaf Shaheed
Alicja Maria Kuberska * Teresa E. Gallion * Noreen Snyder
Michelle Joan Barulich * Shareef Abdur – Rasheed
Ashok K. Bhargava * Elizabeth Castillo * Swapna Behera
Tezmin Ition Tsai * Eliza Segiet * William S. Peters, Sr.

The Year of the Poet XI
July 2024

Featured Global Poets
Barbara Gaiardoni * Bharati Nayak
Errol Bean * Michael Lee Johnson

Renowned Poets

~ Pablo Neruda ~

The Poetry Posse 2024
Gail Weston Shazor * Albert Carasco * Hülya N. Yılmaz
Jackie Davis Allen * Caroline Nazareno * Mutawaf Shaheed
Alicja Maria Kuberska * Teresa E. Gallion * Noreen Snyder
Michelle Joan Barulich * Shareef Abdur – Rasheed
Ashok K. Bhargava * Elizabeth Castillo * Swapna Behera
Tezmin Ition Tsai * Eliza Segiet * William S. Peters, Sr.

The Year of the Poet XI
August 2024

Featured Global Poets
Ibrahim Honjo * Khalice Jade
Irma Kurti * Mennadi Farah

Renowned Poets

~ Li Bai ~

The Poetry Posse 2024
Gail Weston Shazor * Albert Carasco * Hülya N. Yılmaz
Jackie Davis Allen * Caroline Nazareno * Mutawaf Shaheed
Alicja Maria Kuberska * Teresa E. Gallion * Noreen Snyder
Michelle Joan Barulich * Shareef Abdur – Rasheed
Ashok K. Bhargava * Elizabeth Castillo * Swapna Behera
Tezmin Ition Tsai * Eliza Segiet * William S. Peters, Sr.

Now Available
www.innerchildpress.com/the-year-of-the-poet

and there is much, much more !

visit . . .

www.innerchildpress.com/anthologies-sales-special.php

Also check out our Authors and all the wonderful Books Available at :

www.innerchildpress.com/authors-pages

Inner Child Press Anthologies

Now Available

www.worldhealingworldpeacepoetry.com

Inner Child Press Anthologies

Now Available

www.worldhealingworldpeacepoetry.com

www.worldhealingworldpeacepoetry.com

World Healing World Peace
2012, 2014, 2016, 2018, 2020, 2022

Now Available

www.worldhealingworldpeacepoetry.com

Inner Child Press International

'building bridges of cultural understanding'

Meet the Board of Directors

William S. Peters, Sr.
Chair Person
Founder
Inner Child Enterprises
Inner Child Press

Hülya N Yılmaz
Director
Editing Services
Co-Chair Person

Fahredin B. Shehu
Director
Cultural Affairs

Elizabeth E. Castillo
Director
Recording Secretary

De'Andre Hawthorne
Director
Performance Poetry

Gail Weston Shazor
Director
Anthologies

Kimberly Burnham
Director
Cultural Ambassador
Pacific Northwest
USA

Ashok K. Bhargava
Director
WINAwards

Deborah Smart
Director
Publicity
Marketing

www.innerchildpress.com

This Anthological Publication
is underwritten solely by

Inner Child Press International

Inner Child Press is a Publishing Company Founded and Operated by Writers. Our personal publishing experiences provides us an intimate understanding of the sometimes daunting challenges Writers, New and Seasoned may face in the Business of Publishing and Marketing their Creative "Written Work".

For more Information

Inner Child Press International

www.innerchildpress.com

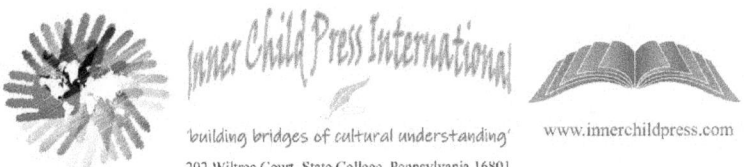

'building bridges of cultural understanding'
202 Wiltree Court, State College, Pennsylvania 16801

www.innerchildpress.com

~ fini ~

www.ingramcontent.com/pod-product-compliance
Lightning Source LLC
LaVergne TN
LVHW051040080426
835508LV00019B/1627